XFORD
IVERSITY PRESS

English File

Upper-intermediate

Workbook WITH KEY

fifth
edition

Christina Latham-Koenig   Clive Oxenden
Kate Chomacki   with Jane Hudson

Contents

Welcome to **English File** fifth edition

Student Book

Use your Student Book in class with your teacher.

Workbook

Practise **Grammar**, **Vocabulary**, and **Pronunciation** for every lesson.

Practise the ***Colloquial English*** for every lesson.

Do the ***Can you remember...?*** exercises to check that you remember the Grammar, Vocabulary, and Pronunciation every two Files.

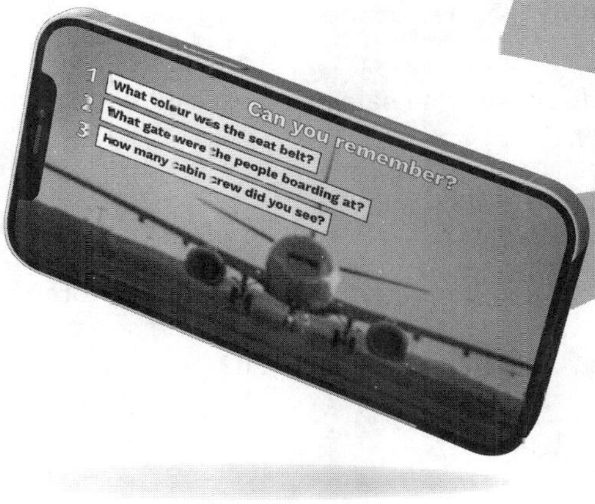

Oxford English Hub

Go to Oxford English Hub (englishhub.oup.com) to:

- Listen to the audio for the Pronunciation exercises.
- Use the Sound Bank videos to practise English sounds.
- Watch the Colloquial English videos before you do the exercises.

1A A tricky question?

G question formation
V understanding idioms and phrasal verbs
P intonation: showing interest

1 GRAMMAR question formation

a Right (✓) or wrong (✗)? Correct the mistakes in the highlighted phrases.

1 **A** You have ever been to Greece?
✗ Have you ever been
B Yes, a couple of times.

2 **A** Why didn't you tell me the truth?
✓
B Because I thought you'd be angry.

3 **A** Where you usually go on holiday?
____
B We usually go to Portugal.

4 **A** Haven't you done the homework?
____
B No, I haven't. I'm sorry.

5 **A** What did happen at the meeting yesterday?
____
B We discussed the sales figures – all very boring, really.

6 **A** Who's Yuki going out with?
____
B She's going out with her best friend's brother.

7 **A** Who repaired your car for you?
____
B My cousin.

8 **A** Whose jacket you did borrow for the wedding?
____
B My dad's. It was a bit big for me.

9 **A** It's late. We should go now?
____
B Yes, we have to get up early tomorrow morning.

10 **A** For who are you waiting?
____
B I'm waiting for my sister.

b Complete the indirect questions and sentences.

1 'Would Michael like this wallet?'
Do you think Michael would like this wallet ?
2 'Where is the lift?'
Could you tell me _______________ ?
3 'Where did we park the car?'
I can't remember _______________ .
4 'Are there any tickets left for the concert tonight?'
Do you know _______________ ?
5 'What time does the match start?'
Can you tell me _______________ ?
6 'When's Fatima's birthday?'
Do you remember _______________ ?
7 'What does Jamie do for a living?'
Do you have any idea _______________ ?
8 'Where does Natalie live?'
I wonder _______________ .
9 'What's Ava's boyfriend's name?'
I'm not sure _______________ .
10 'How much did you pay for your new car?'
Would you mind telling me _______________ ?

c Write the questions.

1 how long / you / spend / in Brazil last summer
How long did you spend in Brazil last summer?
2 who / cook / in your family
____
3 when / your brother / pass / his driving test
____
4 you know / who / go / to the party tonight
____
5 who / the manager / talk to / now
____
6 who / eat / the chocolates / I / leave / in the cupboard
____
7 why / you / not come / to school yesterday
____
8 you remember / what time / the meeting / be
____

d Write questions to ask at a job interview. Use a different phrase to begin each question.

1 salary
____
2 holidays
____
3 working hours
____
4 overtime
____
5 travel
____
6 uniform
____
7 parking space
____
8 lunch
____

2 PRONUNCIATION intonation: showing interest

a 1.2 **Listen to the questions. Tick (✓) if the speaker sounds interested.**

1 Which university did you go to? ✓
2 What don't you like about your job? ☐
3 How's your family? ☐
4 Would you like to work abroad? ☐
5 How many languages do you speak? ☐
6 Why did you leave your last job? ☐

b 1.3 **Listen and repeat the questions with interested intonation.**

c **Complete the table with the expressions and questions in the list.**

~~How interesting!~~ I'm so sorry. Me too! Oh, really? What a shame! Why? Why do you say that? Why is that? Wow!

Expressions showing interest
How interesting!
Expressions showing sympathy
Follow-up questions

d 1.4 **Listen and check. Then listen again and repeat the expressions.**

e 1.5 **Now listen to the questions from a in conversations. Complete the phrases or questions that people use to react to the answers.**

1 *Me too!* When were you there?
2 _______________ How long have you been there?
3 _______________ I hope it's nothing serious.
4 _______________ What's keeping you here?
5 _______________ That's a lot of languages.
6 _______________ I'm sorry to hear that.

f 1.6 **Listen and repeat the responses. Copy the intonation.**

3 **VOCABULARY** understanding idioms and phrasal verbs

a Complete the sentences with the idioms and phrasal verbs in the list.

~~do the trick~~ have something up your sleeve move on play ball print off stick at

1 If you need something for your papers, a document folder should *do the trick*.
2 In a group interview, it's important to ______ and interact with the other candidates.
3 I found it hard to learn a new language, but I managed to ______ it until I achieved my goal.
4 It's useful to think about your strengths and weaknesses in order to ______ if you are asked about them.
5 After I had done the same job for five years, I felt it was time to ______.
6 Make sure you ______ a copy of your CV to take to the interview with you.

b Read the article quickly. Match the bold idioms and phrasal verbs to definitions 1–8.

1 (*phrasal verb*) choose somebody carefully from a group of people *pick out*
2 (*idiom*) wear clothes suitable for a particular role ______
3 (*idiom*) be useful ______
4 (*phrasal verb*) be noticeable because of being different ______
5 (*idiom*) find out all you need to know ______
6 (*phrasal verb*) be mentioned or discussed ______
7 (*idiom*) avoid ______
8 (*phrasal verb*) make or prepare something ______

Important interview tips

Your CV has got you in the door; now it's time to convince the interviewer you're the best person for the job.

Research the company

Do your homework so you don't give the impression you're looking for any old job. Search the internet and read not only the company's website, but also any news stories that **come up**. Make a list of points you could discuss at the interview and questions you could ask. You want your potential future employer to believe that you have a genuine interest in working for the organization.

Dress smartly

The company's dress code should give you an idea of what to wear at the interview, but in most cases, you will be expected to **look the part**. However, it is not only your clothes you must watch. Think about your body language: do you usually slouch or sit up straight in a chair, or do you sometimes fiddle with a pen? Practise before the day so that you have time to replace any bad habits with positive body language.

Mind your manners

When you get to the interview venue, make sure you greet everyone you meet, including the people in the lift. Offer the interviewer a warm greeting and say 'please' and 'thank you' when appropriate. Not only do you want to show that you would be an invaluable team member, but you also want the interviewer to **pick** you **out** when there may be other candidates who are equally qualified for the job.

Give real examples

You won't be the first candidate the interviewer has met, so you need to **stand out** from the competition. When you are asked about your abilities and experience, **steer clear** of typical answers such as 'I have great communication skills' or 'I'm a people person'. Instead, give real examples of situations where you have demonstrated these qualities and brought about a positive result.

Ask the right questions

Towards the end of the interview, you will be invited to ask your own questions about the job. You'll have that list you **put together** beforehand, but the points on it may already have been covered. Even if the interviewer has been very thorough, you must ask a few questions. This is where your initial research about the company will **come in handy**.

1B We may never know

G auxiliary verbs, *the..., the...* + comparatives
V compound adjectives
P intonation and sentence rhythm

1 GRAMMAR auxiliary verbs

a ~~Cross out~~ **the unnecessary words.**

1 My mum can drive, but my dad can't ~~drive~~.
2 I loved that book, but my wife didn't love that book.
3 You weren't listening to the instructions, but I was listening to the instructions.
4 Some people believe in ghosts, but others don't believe in ghosts.
5 Gina's going to the party, but Jared isn't going to the party.
6 I always lock the front door, but my partner doesn't always lock the front door.
7 I've never been to a nutritionist, but my sister has visited a nutritionist.
8 My friends had already heard the story, but I hadn't already heard the story.

b **Complete the conversations with a question tag or an auxiliary.**

1 **A** I sent you a message last night, but you didn't reply.
B I *did* ______ reply. I texted you straight away.

2 **A** I don't feel like cooking tonight.
B Neither ______ I. Shall we go out for dinner? I'd love a curry.
A So ______ I. Come on. Let's go.

3 **A** I've seen this film before.
B Well, I ______.
A Do you mind if I change channels?
B Yes, I ______ mind! I want to see the end.

4 **A** You're going to Sam's party, ______ you?
B No, I'm not.
A Why not? You haven't had another argument with him, ______ you?
B Yes. We aren't going out together any more.

5 **A** I'll be back a bit late tonight.
B ______ you? Where are you going?
A To a concert with some friends.
B You'll be back before 12.00, ______ you?
A Of course.

6 **A** You couldn't lend me some money, ______ you?
B No, sorry. Why?
A I've spent all my money this month.
B So ______ I!

7 **A** I didn't go out last night.
B Neither ______ I. I was too tired.
A So ______ I!

8 **A** You aren't from round here, ______ you?
B No, I'm from Australia.
A I don't suppose you like the British weather.
B Actually, I ______ like it. I prefer cool weather to hot weather.

c **Respond to the statements with** ***So do I, Neither do I, I do, I don't*****, etc., and say why.**

1 I didn't go out yesterday.
______
2 I love the sea.
______
3 I've never been to India.
______
4 I'd like to go on a safari.
______
5 I wasn't interested in history at school.
______
6 I'm good at languages.
______
7 I can swim quite well.
______
8 I don't do any exercise.
______

2 PRONUNCIATION intonation and sentence rhythm

a 1.7 **Listen and complete the conversations.**

1 **A** You *don't* ________ like the soup, *do* ________ you?
B I *do* ________ like it. It's just that it's very hot.

2 **A** We ________ invited to their wedding.
B ________ you? Neither ________ we.

3 **A** I ________ enjoy that film.
B ________ you? I ________.

4 **A** I ________ always very well behaved as a child.
B ________ you? I ________.

5 **A** You ________ forget to call me, ________ you?
B Of course I ________.

6 **A** I ________ play tennis quite well.
B ________ you? I ________.

b **Listen again and repeat the conversations. Copy the rhythm and intonation.**

3 GRAMMAR IN CONTEXT *the..., the...* + comparatives

Complete the sentences with the comparative form of the adjectives in the list.

big cold difficult ~~early~~ far ~~good~~ high interesting late likely long qualified

1 The *earlier* ________ we set off, the *better* ________ chance we'll have of avoiding the rush-hour traffic.
2 The ________ the class, the ________ the students are to learn something.
3 The ________ you go to bed, the ________ it is to get up in the morning.
4 The ________ north you travel in Canada, the ________ it gets.
5 The ________ the person is for the job, the ________ the salary.
6 The ________ your house, the ________ it takes you to clean it.

4 VOCABULARY compound adjectives

a **Match the definitions to the compound adjectives in the list.**

absent-minded ~~bad-tempered~~ big-headed easy-going good-tempered laid-back narrow-minded open-minded self-centred strong-willed tight-fisted two-faced well-balanced well-behaved

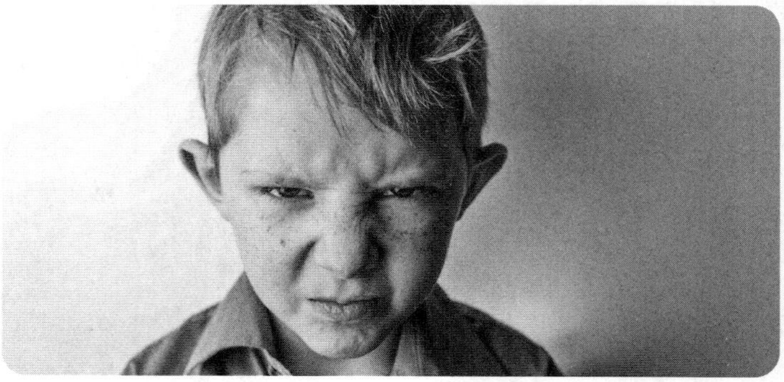

1 easily made angry or annoyed *bad-tempered* ________
2 ready to consider new ideas and opinions ________
3 not willing to spend money ________
4 often forgetting or not noticing things ________
5 determined to do what you want to do, even if other people advise you not to ________
6 relaxed; not easily worried by things ________
7 sensible and emotionally in control ________
8 having a very high opinion of how important and clever you are ________
9 not willing to listen to ideas different from your own ________
10 dishonest about your feelings; telling people what you think will please them ________
11 cheerful and not easily made angry ________
12 thinking only about yourself and not about other people ________
13 calm; not easily upset by what other people do ________
14 behaving in a way that people think is polite and correct ________

b Complete the sentences with the compound adjectives in **a**.

1 My parents are quite *easy-going*__________. They accept most things I do, without getting upset.

2 Yusuf's wife is very ____________________. She doesn't seem to let anything worry her.

3 Oliver's new girlfriend isn't as dramatic as he is. She seems quite ____________________.

4 My partner is quite ____________________. He won't listen to other people's ideas.

5 Irina never thinks of anyone else because she's so ____________________.

6 My brother-in-law is very ____________________. He's nice to me, and then speaks badly of me to other people.

7 Since he went to work abroad for a while, Leo has become more ____________________ about other cultures.

8 She's very ____________________, and if she's decided to become a vegetarian, nothing will stop her.

9 When we go out, my friend Jack never offers to buy the drinks. I wish he wasn't so ____________________.

10 The new manager seems very ____________________. He spent most of the meeting telling us how successful he was.

11 My sister never remembers where she's put her keys. She's very ____________________.

12 I've never seen your children being naughty. They're really ____________________.

13 Our English teacher never seems to get angry. She's extremely ____________________.

14 It's best not to talk to my brother when he first gets up. He's usually very ____________________.

c Choose eight of the compound adjectives in **a** and write sentences about yourself. Explain your answers.

1 ____

2 ____

3 ____

4 ____

5 ____

6 ____

7 ____

8 ____

5 VOCABULARY FROM READING

Complete the missing letters in the words.

1 Detectives are searching for clues to help them *s o* l *v e* last night's murder.

2 She told reporters the ex_ _ _ _ r _ _ n _ _ _ story of how she survived the plane crash.

3 It takes six days to reach the r _ m _ _ _ island of Tristan da Cunha by boat.

4 The search party found no tr_ _ _ of the missing climbers.

5 Nobody knows what happened to the ship, and its fate remains a p_ _ _ l _.

6 The strange geology of the planet Mars continues to b _ f _ _ _ scientists.

COLLOQUIAL ENGLISH 1

English File talks to...
Aasmah Mir
Journalist

1 LOOKING AT LANGUAGE

Match 1–5 to a–e.

1 They said my talk was too long and I should **boil it** _e_
2 I sometimes feel like the examiner is trying to **trip me** ____
3 The news programme had invited an expert to **come** ____
4 You'll find the project more manageable if you **break it** ____
5 With statistics, you have to **cut** ____

a **on** and explain the situation in more detail.
b **down** into separate parts.
c **up** when I'm doing an exam.
d **through** the numbers to learn the important facts.
~~e **down** to about half an hour.~~

2 VOCABULARY FROM THE INTERVIEW

Match definitions 1–7 to a word or phrase from the list.

delivery give sb an easy ride graduate trainee jargon ~~be self-deprecating~~ stay on your brief talk sb's language

1 done in a way that makes your own achievements or abilities seem unimportant _be self-deprecating_
2 make a connection with sb ____________
3 words or expressions used by a particular profession or group ____________
4 make things uncomplicated for sb (*idiom*) ____________
5 sb who has a degree and is being taught how to do a particular job ____________
6 the way sb speaks in public ____________
7 follow your original plans or instructions (*idiom*) ____________

3 THE CONVERSATION

Complete the words to add emphasis in the sentences.

1 It's a terrible, t_errible_ idea to go to an interview when you're feeling hungry.
2 I've d__________ told you this before – in fact I remember mentioning it the last time I saw you.
3 I felt really, r__________ silly when I realized I'd locked my keys in the house.
4 You w__________ make a mistake if you don't practise your speech beforehand.

4 VOCABULARY FROM THE CONVERSATION

Complete the sentences with a word from the list.

caught potentially ~~slightly~~ white willing

1 I sometimes _slightly_ exaggerate when I talk about my experience.
2 You might find yourself in a __________ difficult situation.
3 Nobody will worry if you tell a couple of __________ lies.
4 You could get __________ out if they ask you questions about something on your CV.
5 You need to show that you are __________ to learn.

1 Can you remember...?

GRAMMAR & VOCABULARY

a Complete the second sentence so that it means the same as the first sentence. Use the word in brackets. Contractions are one word.

1 My husband and I both love animals. (so)
I love animals and *so* *does* *my* *husband*.

2 I'm sure I sent you a message last night. (did)
I *did* *send* *you* *a* *message* last night.

3 Whose is this phone? (belong)
Who ______ ______ ______ ______ to?

4 What was wrong with the hotel you stayed in? (like)
Why ______ ______ ______ the hotel you stayed in?

5 Where did you get that book from? (gave)
______ ______ ______ that book?

6 How much is petrol in your country? (costs)
Do you know ______ ______ ______ ______ in your country?

7 Do you have any vacancies at the moment? (whether)
Can you ______ ______ ______ ______ ______ any vacancies at the moment?

8 I'm just checking you'll pick me up from work tonight. (you)
You will pick me up from work tonight, ______ ______?

9 My friends and I can't afford to go on holiday this year. (neither)
I can't afford to go on holiday this year and ______ ______ ______ ______.

10 I'm sure Tom knows about the meeting – he mentioned it yesterday. (does)
Tom ______ ______ ______ ______ ______ – he mentioned it yesterday.

b Read the text. Circle a, b, or c.

The Bermuda Triangle

During the 1960s and 70s, many stories were told of ships and aircraft disappearing mysteriously in a region of the Atlantic Ocean known as the Bermuda Triangle. People asked, '1 ______ is causing these boats and planes to disappear?', and several 2 ______ reasons were given to explain the mystery. Some writers wondered 3 ______ aliens had established an underwater base and were hijacking aircraft to study their crew. Others said that enormous waves might be hitting vessels, causing them to sink without a 4 ______. However, nobody asked the question of whether there really 5 ______ any mystery to explain. Journalist Larry Kusche was the first person to do this. He asked questions about the mysterious disappearances which previous writers 6 ______. These writers had simply collected stories that had already been written and repeated them in their own way. Kusche found many mistakes in their stories: in some cases, there was no record of the ships and planes that were said to have been lost, and in others, they had disappeared during 7 ______ bad storms. Kusche pointed out that it was logical that more accidents would occur in the busy Bermuda Triangle than in more 8 ______ areas such as the South Pacific because the more ships there are in an area, the 9 ______ it is for one of them to sink. In the end, Kusche concluded that the explanation for the Bermuda Triangle 10 ______ was neither aliens nor massive waves, but the lack of research done by writers in search of a sensational story.

1	**a** How	**b** What	**c** Which
2	**a** foreign	**b** extraordinary	**c** absent-minded
3	**a** how	**b** whether	**c** where
4	**a** mark	**b** sign	**c** trace
5	**a** is	**b** has	**c** was
6	**a** didn't	**b** hadn't	**c** weren't
7	**a** rather	**b** quite	**c** extremely
8	**a** congested	**b** far	**c** remote
9	**a** likely	**b** more likely	**c** most likely
10	**a** puzzle	**b** quiz	**c** story

2A Call the doctor!

G present perfect simple and continuous
V illnesses and injuries
P /ʃ/, /dʒ/, /tʃ/, and /k/

1 VOCABULARY illnesses and injuries

a Complete the minor illnesses and injuries.

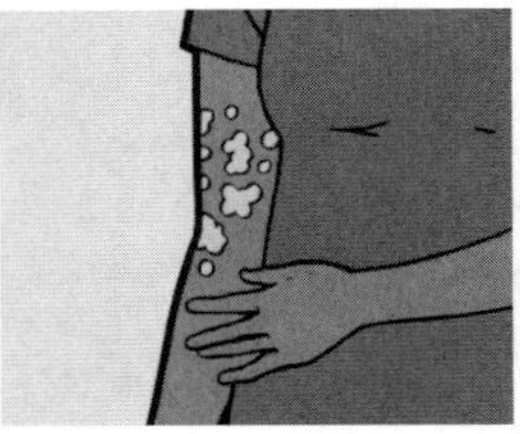

1 She has a r_a_s_h_.

2 She has s___b______.

3 She's b__i____ s______.

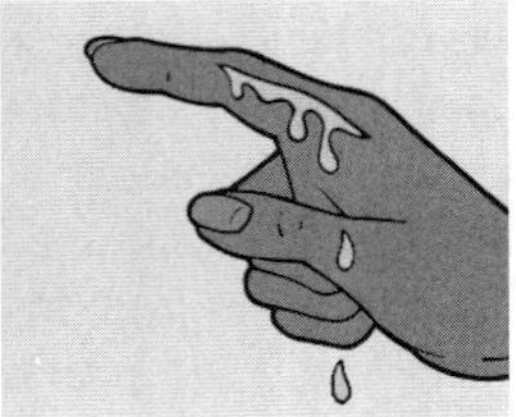

4 Her finger is bl____d______.

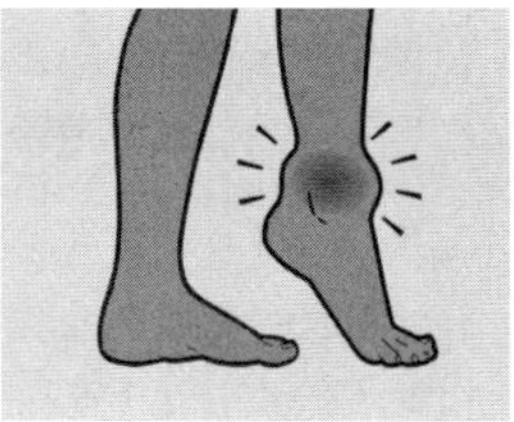

5 Her ankle is s____l____n.

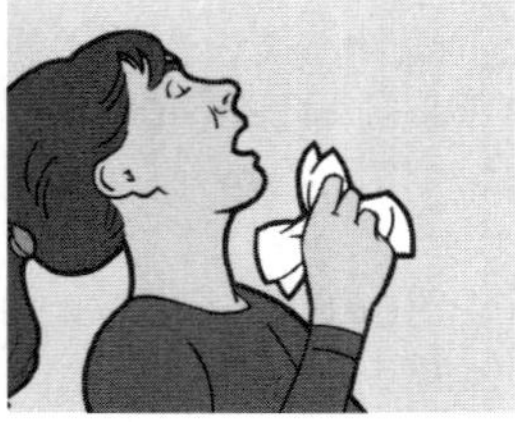

6 She's sn____z______.

7 She's has a c____g__.

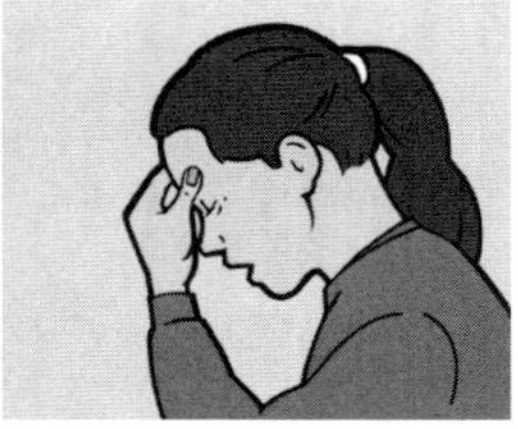

8 She has a h____d__c____.

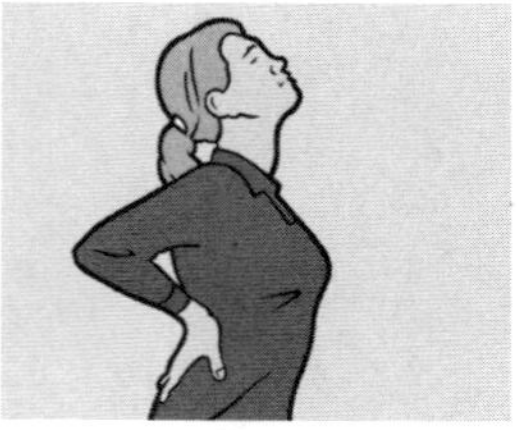

9 Her back h____t__.

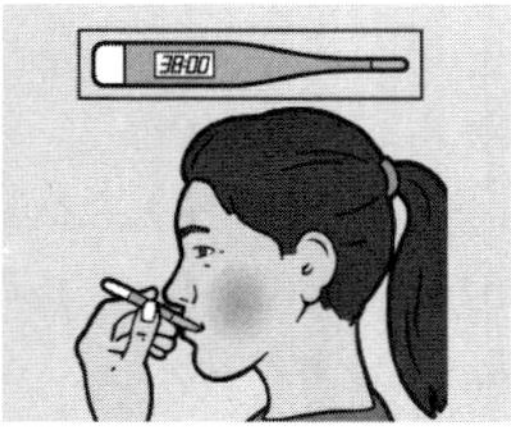

10 She has a t____p__r__t__r__.

b Complete the sentences.

1 Alex has d*iarrhoea*_____. He's been to the toilet six times this morning.

2 I think I have fl__________. I have a temperature and I ache all over.

3 That knife is very sharp. Please don't c__________ y__________.

4 Mateo f__________ in the art gallery. It was so hot that he lost consciousness.

5 These shoes aren't very comfortable. I think I have a bl__________.

6 I have a s__________ thr__________. It hurts when I talk.

7 Amara f__________ s__________. She thinks she's going to vomit.

8 You're coughing and sneezing a lot. Do you have a c__________?

9 I feel d__________. Everything is spinning round.

c Complete the conversations with a word from the list.

~~allergic reaction~~ blood pressure burnt choking food poisoning sprained unconscious

1 **P** There's a rash all over my body.
D You might have had an *allergic reaction* to something.

2 **P** Where am I?
D In hospital. You had an accident and you've been ____________ for an hour.

3 **P** I fell and hurt my wrist playing tennis – now it's very swollen.
D I think you've ____________ it.

4 **P** I sometimes feel a bit dizzy when I first get up.
D It sounds like you have low ____________.

5 **P** I've been sick and I have diarrhoea.
D You might have ____________. Didn't you say you thought the prawns you had for lunch were off?

6 **P** What should I do if one of my children starts ____________?
D Tell them not to panic and to keep coughing – they need to move the food.

7 **P** I dropped a hot pan on my hand.
D Yes, you've ____________ yourself quite badly.

d **Match conditions 1–6 to treatments a–f.**

1 an allergic reaction _e_
2 a headache ____
3 an infection ____
4 a major cut ____
5 a minor cut ____
6 a sprained ankle ____

a have stitches
b put antiseptic cream and a plaster on it
c put ice on it and bandage it
d take antibiotics
~~e take antihistamine tablets or cream~~
f take painkillers

e **Complete the sentences with a word from the list.**

~~down~~ out over round up

1 You should go and lie _down_ if you aren't feeling well.
2 You shouldn't go out until you get ____________ flu properly.
3 If you stand for too long in this heat, you might pass ____________.
4 If you think you're going to throw ____________, tell me and I'll stop the car.
5 I must have fainted. When I came ____________ I was lying on the floor.

f **Complete the medical advice with the words in the list.**

bandage heat pack ice pack ~~pinch~~ push up rub tip

1 You can stop a nosebleed if you _pinch_ the soft part of your nose and ____________ your head forward.
2 Don't use that ____________ for too long because it will make your skin very cold and might cause some damage.
3 You shouldn't put a ____________ on a sprained ankle, as the heat will make the ankle more swollen.
4 Don't ____________ the arms and legs of someone with hypothermia, as you will make them lose more heat.
5 You should only stand behind someone who's choking and ____________ against their stomach if they can't talk, cough, or breathe.
6 If you put antiseptic cream and a ____________ on a bad cut, you will stop the wound getting infected.

g **Write a short paragraph about your last illness / injury. Include...**

- when you were ill / injured and what the illness / injury was.
- what the symptoms were.
- what the treatment was.
- how long it took you to get over it.

2 VOCABULARY FROM READING

Complete the sentences with a phrase from the list.

heart rate life-threatening illness ~~miracle cures~~ open-heart surgery scare stories under the weather worst-case scenario

1 Most stories about _miracle cures_ are fake news.
2 Ahmed is concerned because his ____________ is very fast when he does exercise.
3 Most people want to know about the ____________ when they're diagnosed with an illness, but it's unlikely things will get that bad.
4 It isn't easy for doctors to tell patients that they are suffering from a ____________.
5 I've been feeling ____________ recently, so I've made an appointment with my doctor.
6 My uncle is very ill in hospital, and he's going to have ____________ tomorrow.
7 Newspapers are full of ____________ about what will happen if we eat certain foods.

3 PRONUNCIATION /ʃ/, /dʒ/, /tʃ/, and /k/

a **Circle the word with a different sound.**

ʃ **sh**ower	1 (**ch**est) infec**ti**on pre**ss**ure ra**sh**
k **k**eys	2 a**ch**e **ch**olesterol si**ck** spe**ci**alist
dʒ **j**azz	3 aller**g**ic emer**g**ency fin**g**er in**j**ury
tʃ **ch**ess	4 **ch**oke sti**tch**es stoma**ch** tempera**t**ure
ʃ **sh**ower	5 cou**ch** opera**ti**on **sh**ock uncons**ci**ous
dʒ **j**azz	6 banda**g**e in**j**ection ne**g**ative sur**g**eon

b **2.1 Listen and check. Then listen again and repeat the words.**

4 GRAMMAR present perfect simple and continuous

a Right (✓) or wrong (✗)? Correct the mistakes in the highlighted phrases.

1 You don't need to call the doctor – I've already made an appointment for you.
✓ ______

2 This is the first time I've been spraining my ankle – I didn't know it hurt so much!
✗ I've sprained my ankle ______

3 Mia isn't going to school today because she's been throwing up all night.
______

4 I've fallen over lots of times playing football, but I've never broken a bone.
______

5 I can't take anything for my headache because we've been running out of painkillers.
______

6 You've been complaining about your back for weeks – why don't you go to the doctor's?
______

7 How long have you been knowing about your grandfather's illness?
______

8 Sasha's coughed all day, and now he has a sore throat.
______

9 My sister has a skin problem – she's been going to the hospital for treatment for over two years.
______

10 How many times have you been fainting recently?
______

b Complete the sentences using the words in brackets. Use the present perfect simple or continuous form of the verb. Put the adverbs in the correct position.

1 Evie is a bit nervous – she's never ridden a horse before. (she / ride / never)
2 How many biscuits ______? (you / eat)
3 My brother's really stressed about work, so ______ very well recently. (he / not sleep)
4 ______ my hand on the oven – it really hurts! (I / burn / just)
5 ______ problems with my shoulder for several months now. (I / have)
6 Ed is one of the nicest people ______. (I / meet / ever)
7 ______ to the gym for long – just a few weeks. (Georgia / not go)
8 ______ a sore throat for more than a week now. (Jamie / have)
9 How long ______ a job? (your girlfriend / look for)
10 I bought that book last month, but ______ it yet. (I / not read)

c Complete the email with the correct form of the verbs in brackets. Use the present perfect simple or continuous.

Hi Nicola,

Thanks for your email – it was great to hear from you!

Sorry I [1] haven't replied (not reply) until now, but I [2] ______ (not feel) very well recently. I [3] ______ (have) flu, and I'm only just getting over it now. I [4] ______ (not go) to work for a week; I [5] ______ (lie) on the sofa at home all day. My mum [6] ______ (look after) me all week, and I'm nearly better now. I'll probably go back to work the day after tomorrow.

Anyway, I'm so glad you're planning on coming to visit next summer – it will be lovely to see you! While I've been off work, I [7] ______ (think) about what we can do while you're here, and I [8] ______ (come up with) a few ideas. I know how much you love music, so for the last few days I [9] ______ (try) to get some tickets for a music festival, but I [10] ______ (not manage) to get any yet. Is there anything else you'd like to do during your visit? I'm really looking forward to seeing you, and I know that we'll have a fantastic time.

Write back soon!

Love,

Sophie xx

d Answer Sophie's email. Write 140–190 words. Use the present perfect simple and continuous. Include the following:

- thank Sophie for her email
- explain why you haven't written until now
- answer Sophie's question
- ask Sophie a question

2B You're never too old...

G adjective order before nouns
V clothes and fashion
P vowel sounds

1 VOCABULARY clothes and fashion

a Circle the correct adjective.

1 a *patterned* / *plain* / *striped* T-shirt

2 a *hooded* / *polo-neck* / *tight* jumper

3 a *sleeveless* / *long-sleeved* / *V-neck* T-shirt

4 a *checked* / *plain* / *spotted* shirt

5 a *loose* / *polo-neck* / *tight* T-shirt

6 a *plain* / *checked* / *patterned* shirt

7 a *spotted* / *striped* / *long-sleeved* T-shirt

8 a *loose* / *tight* / *hooded* T-shirt

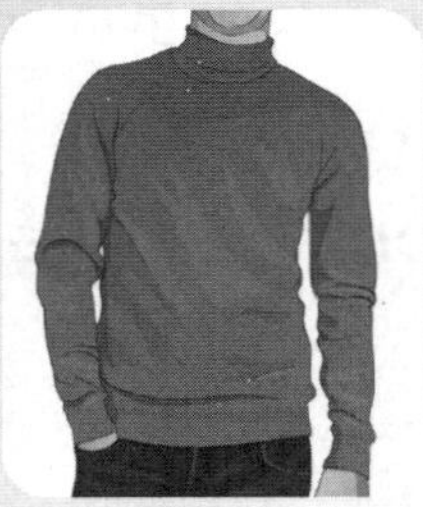

9 a *polo-neck* / *sleeveless* / *patterned* top

10 a *hooded* / *V-neck* / *checked* T-shirt

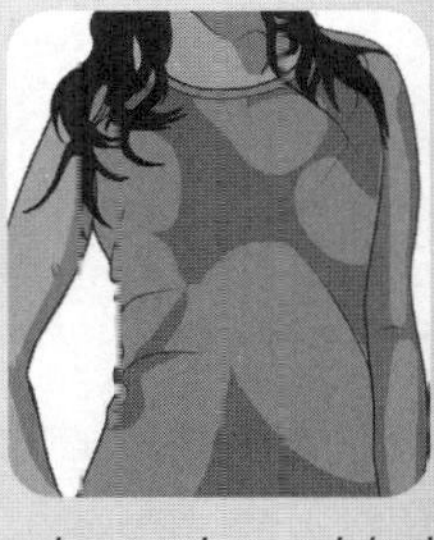

11 a *long-sleeved* / *plain* / *sleeveless* T-shirt

12 a *checked* / *striped* / *loose* T-shirt

b Complete the words for materials.

1 Jack was wearing a blue d_e_n_i_m_ jacket.
2 I prefer to wear light c___t___ ___ ___ shirts in the summer.
3 I gave my mum a blouse with a l___c___ collar for her birthday.
4 Are you sure those boots are made of l___ ___t___ ___ ___?
5 I never buy l___n___ ___ clothes because they take so long to iron.
6 They gave me a very expensive s___ ___k tie as a leaving present.
7 Don't wear your s___ ___d___ jacket outside – it's raining.
8 I really like your new v___ ___v___ ___ jacket. It looks very soft.
9 My aunt often wears a f___ ___ coat, but it isn't real.
10 I always wear a L___c___ ___ top in the gym – it's the most comfortable.
11 My sister wears an old w___ ___l___ ___ ___ cardigan around the house in the winter.

c Complete the sentences.

1 I don't have to wear a uniform at work, but I have to look sm*art*_______ .
2 Alice enjoys wearing cl__________ clothes that will never go out of fashion.
3 It isn't a formal dinner, so I'm going to wear something c__________.
4 Zach looked quite scr__________ when I saw him: his T-shirt was dirty, and he hadn't combed his hair.
5 You look like my dad in those trousers – they're really o__________-f__________.

d Match 1–8 to a–h to make questions.

1 How often do you dress _*f*_
2 How many clothes do you have ___
3 Do you get ___
4 When do you get dressed ___
5 Do you always hang ___
6 What colour do you think ___
7 Is it important for you that your shoes ___
8 Do you have any clothes that go ___

a suits you best?
b in the morning?
c match your clothes? Why (not)?
d that don't fit you?
e with everything? What?
~~f up to go out for a special occasion?~~
g changed as soon as you get home from work / school? Why (not)?
h up your clothes before you go to bed?

e Answer the questions in **d**.

1 ______________________________
2 ______________________________
3 ______________________________
4 ______________________________
5 ______________________________
6 ______________________________
7 ______________________________
8 ______________________________

2 PRONUNCIATION vowel sounds

a Circle the word with a different sound.

 b**oo**t	1 l**oo**se sc**r**u**ff**y (circled) sh**oe**s s**ui**t
 f**i**sh	2 l**i**nen s**i**lk sl**i**ppers str**i**ped
 b**ir**d	3 f**ur** sh**ir**t sh**or**ts sk**ir**t
 b**i**ke	4 f**i**t L**y**cra st**y**lish t**igh**t
 tr**ai**n	5 l**a**ce l**ea**ther pl**ai**n s**ue**de

b 2.2 Listen and check. Then listen again and repeat the words.

3 GRAMMAR adjective order before nouns

a Circle the correct answers.

1 I often wear *loose linen* / *linen loose* clothes in the summer to try to keep cool.
2 I'm looking for a top to match my *red tight* / *tight red* jeans.
3 She bought a *cheap Lycra* / *Lycra cheap* swimsuit in the sales.
4 You'd look great in that *checked long* / *long checked* coat!
5 Are you going to wear your *brand new purple* / *purple brand new* boots tonight?
6 My partner's got a *grey stylish* / *stylish grey* suit he can wear to his brother's wedding.
7 You'll ruin your *suede blue* / *blue suede* shoes if you wear them out in the rain.
8 He wore a *red smart* / *smart red* bow tie to the wedding.

b Rewrite the sentences with the word in brackets in the correct position.

1 What do you think of these striped socks? (long)
What do you think of these long striped socks?

2 I'm looking for a black dress. (classic)

3 He often wears a long-sleeved shirt. (checked)

4 They gave me a beautiful lace top. (French)

5 Have you got a yellow T-shirt I can borrow? (plain)

6 This hooded jacket is on offer. (pink)

7 I'm not a fan of polo-neck sweaters. (tight)

8 Vincent is the one in the fur hat. (strange)

c Right (✓) or wrong (✗)? Correct the mistakes in the highlighted phrases.

1 Sarah's wearing a denim short skirt.
✗ a short denim skirt

2 I'm looking for a sleeveless cotton T-shirt.
✓

3 I want to buy some leather white trousers.

4 You can't wear those old scruffy jeans to the wedding.

5 He gave his mother a spotted silk scarf for her birthday.

6 He looks very smart in his grey new Armani suit.

7 She was wearing a bright red woollen jumper.

8 My sister's bought some purple trendy glasses.

d Write each pair of sentences as one sentence.

1 My grandparents live in an old Victorian house. It's big.
My grandparents live in a big old Victorian house.

2 I met a French woman at the party. She was interesting.

3 My sister has lovely black hair. It's long.

4 Ava's just bought an expensive silk top. It's striped.

5 There's a round wooden table in my friend's kitchen. It's beautiful.

6 Max gave his girlfriend an unusual ring for her birthday. It's gold.

7 My boss drives a powerful Italian sports car. It's red.

8 We've been having some wet weather recently. It's been awful.

3A Flight plan

G narrative tenses, past perfect continuous, *so / such...that...*
V air travel
P irregular past forms, sentence rhythm

1 VOCABULARY air travel

a Replace the **bold** words with a formal word or phrase from the list.

approximately disembark locate ~~personal electronic devices~~ place proceed to rear requiring

1 **Mobile phones**, **tablets**, **and laptops** may be used in flight mode during the flight. *personal electronic devices*
2 There are toilets at the front and at the **back** of the plane. ________
3 Our flight time today is **about** two and a half hours. ________
4 The crew will be passing through the cabin with landing cards for any passengers **needing** one. ________
5 Passengers to New York are asked to **go to** Gate 36 immediately. ________
6 Please check you have all your belongings with you before you **leave the plane**. ________
7 We ask that you **put** bags and jackets under the seat in front of you. ________
8 Please take some time now to **find** your nearest emergency exit. ________

b Circle the correct words.

1 They had booked an economy flight, so they couldn't use the *airport terminal* / *VIP lounge*.
2 It didn't take long for me to check in my suitcase at the *bag drop* / *security*.
3 The passengers were stopped at *customs* / *the check-in desk* for their bags to be checked.
4 I showed my boarding pass and ID at the *baggage reclaim* / *gate* and went to board my flight.
5 I didn't have a boarding pass, so I had to queue at the *check-in desk* / *customs* to get one.
6 We could see our plane on the *runway* / *gate* while we were waiting to board.
7 We parked as near as possible to the *airport terminal* / *VIP lounge* because we were late.
8 The quickest way to find your flight on the departures board is to look at the *flight times* / *runway*.
9 I was wearing boots, so I had to take them off at *security* / *bag drop*.
10 When I went to *baggage reclaim* / *flight times*, I found that my suitcase hadn't arrived.

c Complete the sentences with a word from the list.

arrivals ~~business class~~ collect delayed first class illegal goods luggage trolley

1 Companies often pay for employees to travel *business class*.
2 If your suitcase has wheels, you don't need to use a ________.
3 There's usually a line of taxis waiting outside ________.
4 Passengers who are travelling ________ sit in the most comfortable seats on the plane.
5 You should always keep your ________ with you when you're in an airport.
6 Customs officers check travellers' bags to make sure they are not trying to bring ________ into the country.
7 It can sometimes take a long time to get out of the airport if you have to wait to ________ your bags from baggage reclaim.
8 The departures board informs passengers whether a flight is on time, boarding, closed, or ________.

d Complete the text.

Last year, I wanted to travel from Madrid to Hamburg to visit a friend. I had booked an [1] int*ernational* fl*ight* from Madrid to Frankfurt and a [2] c________ fl________ from Frankfurt to Hamburg. I printed off my [3] b________ p________ the day before my flight, and I took it with me to the airport. I was able to go straight to security in [4] D________ because I only had [5] h________ l________ – a small backpack. After [6] sc________ my bag, they opened it and [7] ch________ it to make sure I wasn't carrying any [8] l________ or [9] sh________ ob________, like scissors. When I finally got my bag back, I looked at the [10] d________ b________ to see if my flight was already [11] b________. I needn't have worried, because the flight was [12] d________. The plane didn't [13] t________ o________ until two hours later. When I eventually arrived in Frankfurt, I was happy to see that my next flight was [14] o________ t________. However, just before we were due to [15] b________, we were informed that the flight had been cancelled – apparently, planes couldn't [16] l________ in Hamburg because of bad weather. In the end, I finished my journey by train, and I arrived in Hamburg eight hours late!

e Complete the missing letters.

1 I couldn't reach my seat because there were some bags blocking the a_i_ _s_ _l_e.

2 We were the last to leave the plane because we were sitting in the back r___w.

3 They booked a d___ ___ ___ ___t f___ ___ ___ ___t so that they didn't have to change planes.

4 The flight attendant asked me if I had fastened my s___ ___t b___ ___t.

5 It's a l___ ___g-h___ ___l f___ ___ ___ ___t, so we leave Rome at 10.00 a.m. and arrive in Buenos Aires 14 hours later.

6 The c___ ___ ___n c___ ___w demonstrated the safety procedure before we took off.

7 We experienced severe t___ ___ ___ ___ ___ ___ ___ ___e during the flight, and some of the passengers were sick.

8 I'm still suffering from j___t l___g after my flight home from Thailand.

f Circle a, b, or c.

1 I ____ abroad five or six times a year.
a journey **b** travel **c** trip

2 I had a terrible ____ here – the flight was delayed, and then we had a lot of turbulence.
a journey **b** travel **c** trip

3 Is Hannah back from her ____ to South America?
a journey **b** travel **c** trip

4 We have to ____ 400 km if we want to see my grandparents.
a journey **b** travel **c** trip

5 My sister wants to go on a ____ around the world in her gap year.
a journey **b** travel **c** trip

6 My ____ to work takes me about an hour.
a journey **b** travel **c** trip

g Complete the phrasal verbs in the questions with a particle from the list.

in (x2) off (x3) on up (x2)

1 Who **picked** you _up_ from the airport the last time you travelled?

2 When do you usually **check** ________ for a flight?

3 Who usually **drops** you ________ at the airport?

4 Have you ever **filled** ________ an immigration form on a trip? If so, where and when?

5 What's the first thing you do when you **get** ________ a plane?

6 Have you ever **picked** ________ the wrong bag at baggage reclaim?

7 Are you usually in a hurry to **get** ________ the plane at the end of a flight? Why (not)?

8 Do you ever feel nervous when a plane **takes** ________?

h Answer the questions in **g**.

1 ________________
2 ________________
3 ________________
4 ________________
5 ________________
6 ________________
7 ________________
8 ________________

2 VOCABULARY FROM READING

Match definitions 1–8 to the words in the list.

altitude ~~cabin~~ engine evacuation low-cost overhead locker special assistance tail

1 the area for passengers to sit on a plane _cabin_

2 providing something that is cheaper than usual ________________

3 the back part of a plane ________________

4 the act of emptying a place of people because it is not safe for them to be there ________________

5 the height above sea level ________________

6 a service that airports provide to passengers, for example, if they have reduced mobility ________________

7 something that produces power to make a vehicle move ________________

8 a place above your seat in a plane where you can leave your bag ________________

3 GRAMMAR IN CONTEXT *so / such...that...*

Circle the correct word.

1 His suitcase was so / *so much* / *such* heavy that he couldn't pick it up.
2 We had *so* / *such* / *such a* long delay that we missed our connecting flight.
3 There were *so* / *so much* / *so many* people at the airport that there weren't any trolleys left.
4 We flew over *so* / *such* / *such a* lovely countryside that I took some photos from the plane.
5 There was *so* / *so much* / *so many* rain that the road to the airport was flooded.
6 We were sitting in *so* / *so much* / *such* narrow seats on the plane that it was very uncomfortable.
7 The flight attendant spoke *so* / *so much* / *such* softly that I couldn't hear what she was saying.

4 GRAMMAR narrative tenses, past perfect continuous

a Circle the correct verb form. Tick (✓) if both are correct.

1 Tim couldn't close his case because he *had put* / *had been putting* too many clothes in it. ☐
2 She *had worked* / *had been working* for the same airline for eight years before she was promoted. ✓
3 I was delighted when I found my passport. I *had looked* / *had been looking* for it for hours. ☐
4 After I *had picked up* / *had been picking up* my luggage, I took a taxi to my hotel. ☐
5 I *had sat* / *had been sitting* in departures for 20 minutes when I saw that my flight was boarding at a different gate. ☐
6 They *had lived* / *had been living* in Manchester before they moved to Scotland. ☐
7 The passengers were angry because the airline *had cancelled* / *had been cancelling* their flight. ☐
8 I was surprised when I was told that my suitcase was too big: I *had taken* / *had been taking* it for years without having to pay for it. ☐

b Complete the text with the correct form of the verbs in brackets.

My parents [1] had never flown (never fly) before, so they were very nervous when we [2] __________ (arrive) at Heathrow Airport to take our flight to Rome. It [3] __________ (rain), so I [4] __________ (leave) them at the terminal building with instructions to get in the queue at the check-in desk while I [5] __________ (go) to park my car in the long-stay car park. However, when I [6] __________ (get) to the check-in desk myself, they were nowhere in sight. I [7] __________ (look) for them everywhere until it occurred to me it was possible they [8] __________ (already / check in) and they [9] __________ (wait) for me in the departure lounge. This was a real problem for me because I [10] __________ (give) my passport to my mother, so I couldn't check in. I [11] __________ (call) my parents on their phone and, fortunately, my mother answered. They [12] __________ (already / go) through to the departure lounge, and they [13] __________ (wait) for me for nearly half an hour at the gate. Apparently, my mum [14] __________ (read) her book and my dad [15] __________ (do) a crossword. After we hung up, my mum found an understanding member of staff who met me at the information desk with my passport!

c Write a paragraph about an air travel experience you have had. Use narrative tenses.

5 PRONUNCIATION irregular past forms, sentence rhythm

a Write the past simple of the verbs in the list next to the past simple verb that has the same pronunciation of the vowel sound.

~~catch~~ fly meet pay say sing stand tell wake wear

1 bought	caught	6 spoke	__________
2 rang	__________	7 sold	__________
3 made	__________	8 knew	__________
4 let	__________	9 could	__________
5 saw	__________	10 read	__________

b 3.1 Listen and check. Then listen again and repeat the past simple forms.

c 3.2 Listen and complete the gaps in the anecdote.

We were on a [1] flight to **Tokyo**, and we'd been [2] __________ for about [3] __________ **hours**. I was **listening** to [4] __________, and my [5] __________ was **sleeping**, when [6] __________ we **heard** a **very loud** [7] __________. It [8] __________ as if an **engine** had **exploded**. The [9] __________ **didn't tell** us what had [10] __________ until **half** an **hour later**.

d Listen again and practise reading the anecdote aloud with the right rhythm.

3B A twist in the tale

G the position of adverbs and adverbial phrases
V adverbs and adverbial phrases
P word stress and intonation

1 GRAMMAR the position of adverbs and adverbial phrases

a Circle the adverb or adverbial phrase that is different.

1 **time** afterwards (indoors) soon tonight
2 **place** here in fact at home outside
3 **manner** absolutely fluently gracefully slowly
4 **degree** a bit almost hard very
5 **comment** clearly fortunately obviously sometimes
6 **frequency** always rarely normally straight away

b Re-order the words to make sentences. Put the adverb in its usual position.

1 I / umbrella / an / had / luckily / taken
Luckily, I had taken an umbrella.
2 ill / hardly ever / daughter / is / my
______
3 parents / next year / are / his / retiring
______
4 boy / rude / teacher / was / to / the / extremely / his
______
5 dresses / my / stylishly / very / sister
______
6 is / James / apparently / divorced / getting
______
7 were / would / you / never / thought / I / have / 30
______
8 bandaged / was / by a nurse / his ankle / carefully
______
9 be / in five minutes / I'll / there
______
10 go / much / the / to / later / in / I / summer / bed
______

c In each sentence one of the highlighted adverbs or adverbial phrases is in the wrong position. Rewrite the sentences.

1 He usually immediately gets up when his alarm rings.
He usually gets up immediately when his alarm rings.
2 Although she studies a lot, she goes rarely to the library.
______
3 I crashed my new car unfortunately last week.
______
4 Ideally, we should leave tomorrow early.
______
5 I can understand a word hardly when people speak English quickly.
______
6 Kevin nearly forgot yesterday his doctor's appointment.
______
7 She's angry incredibly because her husband came home late last night.
______
8 It surprisingly didn't rain at all while we were in London.
______

2 **VOCABULARY** adverbs and adverbial phrases

a **Circle the correct word.**

1 Ellie ate all her lunch, *ever* / *even* the vegetables!
2 I haven't seen Jian *late* / *lately* – have you?
3 I can't stand most TV programmes, *specially* / *especially* reality shows.
4 Dave *near* / *nearly* crashed his car, but he braked just in time.
5 Please don't tell me what happens because I haven't read the book *still* / *yet*.
6 I'm not going to Irina's party. I *hard* / *hardly* know her! She's your friend, not mine.
7 Do you *ever* / *even* wear jeans to work?
8 My grandparents don't live *near* / *nearly* here; they live about 30 miles away.
9 My father worked very *hard* / *hardly* all his life.
10 Alan's feet are so big that his shoes are *especially* / *specially* made for him.
11 My cousin is a doctor, and *at the moment* / *actually* she's working in Nigeria.
12 I can't wait to find out what happens *at the end* / *in the end* of this book.
13 I missed my bus because I got up *late* / *lately*.
14 We were thinking of going to the cinema, but *at the end* / *in the end* we just went out for a drink.
15 I thought the film was going to be boring, but *actually* / *at the moment* I really enjoyed it.
16 I didn't finish the exam – I was *still* / *yet* writing when the teacher told us to stop.

b **Complete the sentences with an adverb from the list that matches the definition in brackets.**

apparently ~~basically~~ certainly eventually gradually ideally in fact obviously

1 *Basically* __________ (the main reason is), we haven't got enough money to buy our own flat.
2 __________ (in a perfect world), we'd each have our own room in the flat, but that isn't possible.
3 That's __________ (without a doubt) the best lobster that I've ever eaten – it was delicious!
4 My sister is __________ (little by little) building a new life for herself after her divorce.
5 If you keep applying for jobs, you'll find one __________ (in the end).
6 I thought the meal was going to be expensive, but __________ (the truth is) it was quite reasonable.
7 __________ (clearly), her son will move out when he gets a job, but for now he's living with her.
8 __________ (according to what I've heard), a lot of flights have been cancelled because of the cabin crew strike.

c **Complete the stories with the adverbs from the lists. There are one or two adverbs in each list that you don't need to use.**

EVOLUTION

~~every day~~ fast harder hardly ever one day

She ran [1] *every day* __________.
She ran far, ran [2] __________.
She pushed her body to its physical limits.
[3] __________, she felt compelled
to run farther, faster, [4] __________.
And she did.
She ran till her body tingled, until she was wind,
and crimson wings erupted from her back.
Then she flew.

Love at first flight

alone at long last eagerly probably very

Jamie knew her match was out there,
[5] __________ traveling first class.
[6] __________, she flew Milwaukee
to Chicago, but her seatmate was old and
boring. She sat [7] __________ in
first class Chicago to Orlando.
[8] __________ Jamie met her
Mr. Right, working at the ticket counter
of her local airport.

Generation gap

always angrily extremely unfortunately

He was worried. [9] ________________, since his wife's death, his teenage daughter had become [10] ________________ difficult. They had agreed 2.00 a.m. as the latest return time from nightclubs. Now it was 3.30. He prepared himself for confrontation as the door opened. 'Dad!' she shouted [11] ________________. 'I've been frantic. You're late again.'

Trading places

actually enviously suddenly together

We were having breakfast [12] ________________ – I at my table and he at the feeder outside of the window.

For a long moment we gazed [13] ________________ at each other. I said, 'If only I could fly in the air,' to which he replied, 'If only I could sit in a chair.'

d **Choose six adverbs or adverbial phrases from the list and write sentences that are true for you.**

a lot apparently fluently here ideally incredibly slowly sometimes tonight usually

1 ________________
2 ________________
3 ________________
4 ________________
5 ________________
6 ________________

3 PRONUNCIATION word stress and intonation

a **Underline the stressed syllable in the adverbs in the list. Then put them in the correct column.**

~~ab|so|lute|ly~~ ac|tua|lly a|ppa|rent|ly ba|si|ca|lly de|fi|nite|ly e|spe|cia|lly e|ven|tua|lly for|tu|nate|ly gra|dua|lly i|dea|lly in|cre|dib|ly lu|cki|ly ob|vi|ous|ly un|for|tu|nate|ly

Stress on first syllable	Stress on second syllable	Stress on third syllable
		absolutely

b 🔊 **3.3** **Listen and check. Then listen again and repeat the adverbs.**

c 🔊 **3.4** **Listen and complete the sentences.**

1 I absolutely love Japanese food, especially sushi.
2 I thought Brad was single, but ________ he's ________.
3 We paid a lot for the tickets, but ________, the play was ________ boring.
4 That film is ________________.
5 I ________ want to change my job, ________ for something better paid.
6 ________, Tina has been made redundant, so she's moving back in with her ________.

d **Listen again and repeat the sentences. Copy the stress and intonation of the adverbs.**

English File talks to…

Joseph Coelho

Author

1 LOOKING AT LANGUAGE

Complete the common expressions in the conversations.

1 **A** Did you read all the books in the series?
B Yes, I really kept **d**iving________ **back into** the story as each book was published.

2 **A** What do you enjoy most about reading?
B I love learning about places **beyond my d**____________.

3 **A** If someone gives you a book as a present, do you feel obliged to read it?
B No, I think **choice is k**____________. I'll only read a book if I want to.

4 **A** How often do you read?
B Before I go to sleep, so **on a daily b**____________, really.

5 **A** Do you regret spending so much time reading as a child?
B Not at all. I think it **broadened my h**____________.

6 **A** Why did you like that book so much?
B It's difficult to **put into w**____________ how much I loved the story and the characters.

2 VOCABULARY FROM THE INTERVIEW

Complete the sentences from the interview with a word or phrase from the list.

convey a meaning   creepy   fairy tales   illustrations   ~~is taken by~~   pastime   wannabe

1 If a young person is taken by__ a poem and they want to learn it, brilliant.
2 It might mean putting on a different accent, using different types of voices to ______________.
3 I think it becomes more difficult for them to see that reading is an enjoyable ______________.
4 It's really important for any ______________ writers out there to get into the habit of recording ideas when they arise.
5 I caught up and discovered a love for reading and was really into ______________.
6 When I was young, ______________ were just as important as the words.
7 But I loved them because they were a little bit ______________.

3 THE CONVERSATION

Complete the vague language in the sentences.

1 You can just kind________ of__________ lose yourself in this imaginary world.
2 I'm into non-fiction: biographies, memoirs a__________ th__________ l__________ th__________.
3 It's just something I s__________ o__________ grew up with.
4 I don't know that I would, l__________, recommend it to anyone.

4 VOCABULARY FROM THE CONVERSATION

Replace the *italic* words with a word or phrase from the list.

a clue   huge   key to   out of it   ~~tough~~

1 It's really *difficult*. tough________
2 I haven't got *any idea*. ____________
3 I feel a little *bit disconnected*. ____________
4 It's *so big*. ____________
5 That's the *critical thing about* any good book. ____________

GRAMMAR & VOCABULARY

a Complete the sentences with the correct form of the **bold** word.

1 I don't agree with my brother's ________________ views. He refuses to listen to other people's opinions. **MIND**

2 Your wrist is quite ________________ – I think you might have sprained it. **SWELL**

3 Andrea is taking antibiotics because she has a nasty throat ________________. **INFECT**

4 Matt was ________________ relieved when he found out he'd passed his driving test. **INCREDIBLE**

5 My shoulders got sunburnt because I was wearing a ________________ dress. **SLEEVE**

6 She tends to wear clothes that are practical rather than ________________. **FASHION**

7 There was a long queue at ________________ because only one of the scanning machines was working. **SECURE**

8 My dad's picking me up from the airport – he said he'd wait for me in ________________. **ARRIVE**

9 We had some shelves ________________ made for the space between the cupboard and the window. **SPECIAL**

10 Living on my own felt strange to start with, but I'm ________________ getting used to it. **GRADUAL**

b Read the article. Circle a, b, or c.

LUCKY ESCAPE AT TRABZON AIRPORT

Can you imagine how [1]____ if you were on a plane that slid off the runway when it landed? This is exactly what happened on a domestic flight in Türkiye one evening in January 2018. The plane had [2]____ without incident from the capital, Ankara, and the flight had continued as normal. However, the pilot got into difficulties as he [3]____ in Trabzon, in the north-east of the country. Bad weather in the area [4]____ the runway to become very wet. The runway was [5]____ slippery that when the Boeing 737-800 landed, the wheels began to slide. The pilot tried to correct the mistake, but he [6]____. The plane slid off the tarmac and started going towards the cliffs above the Black Sea. [7]____, the wheels got stuck in the mud on the side of the cliffs, and the plane stopped before it reached the sea. At the time, there were 168 people on board: 162 passengers, two pilots, and four cabin [8]____. Fortunately, they only had to wait 20 minutes for the emergency services to arrive and help them [9]____ the plane. The injured passengers were taken to hospital immediately, but they were all sent home within a very short time. Psychologists said it may take time for some of the passengers to [10]____ the shock.

1	**a** did you feel	**b** you would feel	**c** would you feel
2	**a** dropped off	**b** picked up	**c** taken off
3	**a** landed	**b** had landed	**c** was landing
4	**a** caused	**b** had caused	**c** had been causing
5	**a** so	**b** so much	**c** such
6	**a** couldn't	**b** hadn't	**c** wasn't
7	**a** Ideally	**b** Luckily	**c** Obviously
8	**a** staff	**b** attendants	**c** crew
9	**a** get out	**b** get away	**c** get off
10	**a** come round	**b** get over	**c** pass out

4A Riding the storm

G future perfect and future continuous
V weather
P vowel sounds

1 GRAMMAR future perfect and future continuous

a Circle the correct form.

1 Hopefully, we *will be saving* / *will have saved* enough money to go on holiday by the summer.

2 This time tomorrow, we *will be travelling* / *will have travelled* to Scotland – it's an eight-hour journey, so take something to do on the train.

3 I *won't have finished* / *won't be finishing* the report by Friday – can I give it to you on Monday morning?

4 Don't phone between one and two o'clock because we *will have had* / *will be having* lunch.

5 We *will have had* / *will be having* five meetings by the end of today.

6 Jack *will be leaving* / *will have left* for Mexico on Saturday. I'm taking him to the airport.

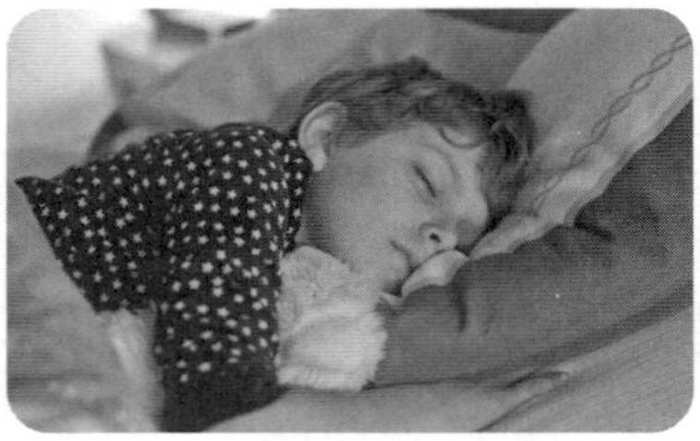

7 I won't see my children tonight – they *will be going* / *will have gone* to bed by the time I get home.

8 I've organized a surprise party for Alex – when we get to the restaurant, all her friends *will be waiting* / *will have waited* for her!

b Complete the sentences with the future perfect or future continuous form of the verb in brackets.

1 By the end of this month, we*'ll have moved* (move) house, so you can come and stay.
2 This time tomorrow, my parents ________ (fly) over the Atlantic on their way to Boston.
3 My exams are in May, so I ________ (do) them all by 1st June.
4 Hopefully, you ________ (read) the book I lent you by the next time I see you.
5 If the match starts at 7.00 p.m., we ________ (play) until 8.45 at least.
6 In a year's time, they ________ (build) the new road, and we'll be able to get to work much quicker.
7 When do you think you ________ (finish) paying your mortgage?
8 Don't call me tomorrow morning because I ________ (drive) to Manchester.
9 It's been raining all morning, but hopefully it ________ (stop) by this afternoon.
10 ________ (you go) to the supermarket later?

c Write future perfect or future continuous questions.

1 when / you / have / your next holiday
When will you be having your next holiday?
2 what / you / do / this time tomorrow
____
3 what time / you / get up / tomorrow morning
____
4 how much TV / you / watch / by the end of the week
____
5 where / you go / next weekend
____
6 when / you / finish / your English homework
____
7 how many times / you / look at your phone / by the end of today?
____
8 how many hours / you / spend / study English / by the end of the week
____

d Answer the questions in **c**.

1 ______________________________

____

2 ______________________________

____

3 ______________________________

____

4 ______________________________

____

5 ______________________________

____

6 ______________________________

____

7 ______________________________

____

8 ______________________________

____

2 VOCABULARY weather

a Circle the word that is different.

1 below zero cold cool mild
2 damp drizzling drought humid
3 boiling freezing hot scorching
4 breeze chilly hurricane windy
5 changeable fog mist smog
6 pouring showers warm wet

b Complete the sentences.

1 We're having a h*eatwave*. It isn't usually so hot at this time of year.
2 Many drivers had to spend the night in their vehicles after they were caught in the bl__________ and their cars got stuck in the snow.
3 People say that there may be a fl__________ if the river continues rising.
4 In some areas, there was h__________. The balls of ice were enormous!
5 Last night, there was a violent storm and the sound of th__________ woke me up.
6 The government wants us to save water because of the dr__________.
7 In India, the m__________ usually lasts until September. The rain can be very heavy.
8 The l__________ lit up the sky during the thunderstorm.
9 Hundreds of trees blew down in the h__________, and several buildings were damaged.

c Match 1–9 to a–i.

1 Everyone is hoping for clear *c*
2 They said the weather will be changeable, ____
3 There were so few sunny ____
4 The forecast is for heavy ____
5 Planes can't take off in this thick ____
6 Driving will be dangerous this morning because of the icy ____
7 Most parts of the country will enjoy bright ____
8 Many trees were blown down by strong ____
9 We hope the weather will be more settled ____

a roads, so drivers should take care.
b next week – we're going on a cruise.
~~c skies so that they can see the solar eclipse.~~
d sunshine today, and it will be quite warm.
e rain, so the barbecue has been cancelled.
f winds during last night's storm.
g so I'm taking my sunglasses and an umbrella.
h fog, so several flights have been cancelled.
i periods that we didn't spend much time at the beach.

d Complete the paragraphs with the words in each list.

~~freezing~~ hail heavy icy strong

January is one of the coldest months in the UK. The temperature sometimes drops to 0°C, so it's [1] *freezing* outside, and the roads are [2] ____________. There are often [3] ____________ winds and [4] ____________ rain; during some storms, [5] ____________ may fall instead of rain.

breeze changeable mild showers sunny

In April, it isn't as cold, and some days can be quite [6] ____________ – around 16°C. There are often rain [7] ____________, with [8] ____________ periods between them because the weather is very [9] ____________. There's often a [10] ____________, which can sometimes be quite cool.

bright cool drizzling settled warm

In July, the weather still isn't [11] ____________, and it continues to change a lot: one minute there's [12] ____________ sunshine, and the next it rains. The rain isn't usually heavy; it's often [13] ____________. In general, it's [14] ____________ during the day – around 20°C – but it can get [15] ____________ in the evenings, so you need a light jacket.

chilly clear damp mist pours

By October, the temperature starts to fall again, and it can be quite [16] ____________ outside – only 5°C or 6°C. Some mornings start out with [17] ____________ in the mountains and near the sea, while on others there are [18] ____________ skies and you can see for a long way. Towards the end of the autumn, the weather can be rather [19] ____________, and it often [20] ____________ with rain.

e Write a paragraph about the weather in your country in January, April, July, and October.

____

____

____

____

____

____

____

____

____

3 PRONUNCIATION vowel sounds

a Circle the word with a different sound.

tree	1 breeze freezing (great) heatwave
boot	2 cool flood monsoon typhoon
bike	3 bright icy lightning mist
owl	4 blow drought shower towel
fish	5 blizzard chilly drizzling mild
up	6 humid hurricane sunny thunder
ear	7 clear here wear zero
egg	8 heat heavy sweat weather
horse	9 scorching storm warm world
phone	10 although below pouring snow

b 4.1 Listen and check. Then listen again and repeat the words.

4B At your own risk

G zero and first conditionals, future time clauses
V expressions with *take*
P linked phrases

1 GRAMMAR zero and first conditionals, future time clauses

a Complete the sentences with a verb from the list. Decide if they are zero conditional or first conditional sentences. Write 0 (zero) or 1 (first).

are cooks doesn't answer doesn't come ~~don't get~~ eat 'll stay won't move

1 Plants die if they *don't get* __________ enough water. *0*
2 If you __________ too many calories, you put on weight. ____
3 I __________ at a friend's house tonight if I miss the last train. ____
4 My sister __________ her phone if she's watching a film on TV. ____
5 Some dogs bite if they __________ scared. ____
6 If we don't sell our house, we __________. ____
7 If Jamal __________ dinner tonight, Yolanda will be delighted. ____
8 If the bus __________ soon, I'll get a taxi. ____

b Complete the sentences with the correct form of the verb in brackets.

1 *Bring* __________ your swimsuit if you want to use the pool. (bring)
2 If my husband __________ home before 7.30, he gets caught in the rush hour traffic. (not leave)
3 It's raining. You'll get wet if you __________ an umbrella with you. (not take)
4 Don't interrupt Kiara if she __________. (study)
5 If you __________ 18 or over, you can vote in a general election. (be)
6 If you can't take me to the airport, I __________ a friend. (ask)
7 If you __________ Jessie Burton's new book yet, I'll buy you a copy for your birthday. (not read)
8 If I __________ eight hours' sleep, I always feel awful the next day. (not get)

c Complete the second sentence so that it means the same as the first sentence. Use a time expression from the list and no more than two other words.

~~after~~ as soon as before if in case unless until when

1 I'll do my Pilates, and then I'll have a shower.
I'll have a shower *after I do* __________ my Pilates.
2 My boyfriend will arrive at his hotel. He'll call me immediately.
My boyfriend will call me __________ at his hotel.
3 We'll arrive in time for lunch if the traffic isn't bad.
We'll arrive in time for lunch __________ is bad.
4 I'm going to call my husband. He might forget his doctor's appointment.
I'm going to call my husband __________ his doctor's appointment.
5 Sarah is going to pack her suitcase. Then she'll go to bed.
Sarah is going to pack her suitcase __________ to bed.
6 We'll wait for you to get home, then we'll have dinner.
We won't have dinner __________ home.
7 I might be late tonight, so don't wait up for me.
Don't wait up for me __________ late tonight.
8 I'll go to New York and I'll stay with some friends.
I'll stay with some friends __________ to New York.

d Complete the sentences about you.

1 I'll have dinner after ______________________________.
2 I'll buy a new car as soon as ______________________________.
3 I won't go to bed tonight until ______________________________.
4 I'll go shopping before ______________________________.
5 I might go out later if ______________________________.
6 I won't move to a new house unless ______________________________.
7 I'll finish my English homework now, in case ______________________________.
8 I'll retire when ______________________________.

2 **PRONUNCIATION** linked phrases

a **4.2** **Listen and complete the sentences.**

1 *First of all*, let's see how much money we've got.
2 I didn't really want to go, but it was ________________ the end.
3 Look smart, ________________, don't be late.
4 ________________ world, everyone would have a roof over their head.
5 Don't disturb me ________________ important.
6 I'll call you ________________ I get home.
7 ________________ I'm concerned, there's nothing more to say.
8 It was ________________ experience that I don't really want to think about it.

b **Listen again and repeat the words. Copy the rhythm.**

3 **VOCABULARY** expressions with *take*

a Match 1–10 to a–j.

1 Grandparents often **take care of** children *e*
2 Don't **take a risk** ____
3 Try to **take** all the factors **into account** ____
4 If you get an interesting job opportunity, ____
5 **Take no notice** of people who shout; ____
6 If you want to be involved in the protest, ____
7 If my children find a baby animal, ____
8 The Olympics **take place** every four years; ____
9 Please don't hurry; ____
10 Climate change is a huge problem; ____

a if you think something bad might happen.
b they're always held in a different country.
c they'll stop if you don't give them your attention.
d **take advantage of** it.
~~e when their parents can't look after them.~~
f before you make a decision.
g we need to **take it seriously**.
h you can **take your time**.
i you can **take part in** the demonstration.
j they always **take pity on** it and give it some food.

b Complete the sentences with the **bold** phrases in **a**.

1 We didn't *take* __________ the rush-hour traffic *into account* __________, so we nearly missed our flight.

2 Why don't we __________ __________ the lovely weather and go to the beach?

3 My children love drama, so they always __________ __________ the school play.

4 This report doesn't need to be finished today – you can __________.

5 Most music festivals __________ __________ in the summer months when it's more likely to be sunny.

6 I always __________ __________ my elderly neighbour when he's ill. I visit him every day to check if he needs anything.

7 The pilot decided to __________ __________ and try to land the plane on the river.

8 Could you __________ __________ my cat while I'm on holiday?

9 __________ of Charlie – he doesn't mean to be rude.

c Match the **bold** phrasal verbs in 1–8 to definitions a–h.

1 When was the last time someone **took** you **out** for dinner? *d*
2 Who was the last person you **took to** immediately? ___
3 Do you **take** your shoes **off** as soon as you go into your house? ___
4 Has anyone you know ever suddenly **taken against** you? ___
5 In what ways do you **take after** your parents? ___
6 How often do you **take** the rubbish **out**? ___
7 Have you ever watched the planes **take off** and land at an airport? ___
8 If you could **take up** a new activity, what would it be? ___

a to leave the ground and begin to fly
b to start not liking somebody for no clear reason
c to remove a piece of clothing
~~d to take somebody to a place and pay for them~~
e to start liking somebody
f to learn or start to do something, especially for pleasure
g to remove something from inside, e.g., a house
h to look or behave like

d Answer the questions in **c** about you.

1 __________
2 __________
3 __________
4 __________
5 __________
6 __________
7 __________
8 __________

Get me out of here!

G unreal conditionals
V feelings
P word stress in three- or four-syllable adjectives

1 VOCABULARY & PRONUNCIATION feelings; word stress

a **Read the questions and complete the missing letters in the answers.**

How would you feel if...

1 someone told you that your new hairstyle didn't suit you? o*f* *f* *e* *n* d *e* *d*
2 you had an argument with your best friend and they said they never wanted to see you again? u___ s___ ___
3 your daughter had just won a painting competition? pr___ ___ ___
4 you thought you'd lost your house keys, then you found them at the bottom of your bag? r___ l___ ___ ___ ___ ___
5 you went camping, it was raining, and everything was soaking wet? m___ s___ r___ ___ ___ ___
6 all your friends were on holiday and you had nobody to talk to? l___ ___ ___ l___
7 you weren't offered a job after you went for the interview? d___ s___ p___ ___ ___ ___ t___ ___
8 you were studying abroad and you were missing your family? h___ ___ ___ s___ ___ ___
9 it was pouring with rain and a friend offered to drive you to your home? gr___ ___ ___ f___ ___
10 your flight had already been delayed three times, then it was cancelled? f___ ___ u___

b Replace the **bold** words with an adjective from the list.

astonished bewildered delighted desperate devastated horrified overwhelmed stunned ~~thrilled~~

1 They're **very excited** to be travelling around South America after saving for so long. *thrilled*
2 When you buy a new phone, it's easy to get **very confused** by all the different options and contracts. ________
3 People were **extremely shocked and disgusted** when they heard about the terrorist attack. ________
4 Andy was **amazed** when his parents gave him a car for his birthday ________
5 She was **so surprised that she couldn't react** when she saw the fire damage. ________
6 Olivia was **incredibly pleased** when she got promoted. ________
7 My brother was **extremely upset** when his wife left him. ________
8 The soldier's wife was **so happy that she didn't know how to react** when her husband suddenly arrived home after six months away. ________
9 The climbers were **losing hope**. It was getting dark, snowing heavily, and they couldn't see a way down the mountain. ________

c Complete the sentences with a word from the list.

~~down~~ gobsmacked gutted scared stiff shattered sick of

1 My uncle was a bit *down* ________ after he lost his job.

2 I'm ________________ always having to work late.

3 My cousin was ________________ when our neighbour's dog started running after her.

4 Hassan couldn't sleep on the flight from New York, so he's absolutely ________________ today.

5 I was totally ________________ when I saw the time – we'd been chatting for nearly two hours!

6 My nephew was ________________ when he didn't get a place at the university he wanted.

d **Underline the stressed syllable in the adjectives in the list. Then put them in the correct column.**

~~a|sto|nished~~ be|wil|dered de|ligh|ted des|pe|rate de|va|sta|ted di|sa|ppoin|ted gob|smacked grate|ful gu|tted home|sick ho|rri|fied lone|ly mise|ra|ble o|ffen|ded o|ver|whelmed re|lieved sha|ttered up|set

Stress on first syllable	Stress on second syllable	Stress on third syllable
	astonished	

e 5.1 **Listen and check. Then listen again and repeat the adjectives. Copy the rhythm.**

f **Choose six feelings in d that you have experienced yourself. Write a sentence about when you experienced each feeling.**

1 ________________

2 ________________

3 ________________

4 ________________

5 ________________

6 ________________

2 GRAMMAR unreal conditionals

a **Circle the correct form.**

1 My colleague *was* / *would be* more popular if he didn't take himself so seriously.
2 I would have got cold if I *didn't take* / *hadn't taken* a jacket.
3 You *hadn't have* / *wouldn't have* sprained your ankle if you'd been looking where you were going.
4 I'd really miss you if you *went* / *would go* to live in London.
5 Vicki *had* / *would have* more friends if she didn't complain all the time.
6 I *had been* / *would have been* really disappointed if I hadn't got the job.
7 He *didn't be able to* / *wouldn't be able to* afford a new car if he wasn't living with his parents.
8 We wouldn't have gone to Thailand in June if we *knew* / *had known* it was the monsoon season.
9 Jacob wouldn't be so stressed if he *had* / *would have* a more understanding boss.
10 We wouldn't have got lost if we *had stayed* / *would have stayed* on the path.

b **Complete the second and third conditional sentences.**

1 We don't go away at the weekend because we don't have much free time.
If we had more free time, we'd go away at the weekend.

2 There wasn't much snow, so we didn't make a snowman.
If there had been more snow, ________________.

3 I didn't know the water was so cold, so I jumped in.
I wouldn't have jumped in if ________________.

4 He doesn't pass his driving test because he gets so nervous.
He would pass his driving test if ________________.

5 We missed the last bus because we left the party too late.
If we'd left the party earlier, ________________.

6 You get sunburnt because you don't use enough sun cream.
If you used more sun cream, ________________.

7 They hadn't read the book, so they didn't really understand the film.
They would have understood the film if ________________.

8 I don't earn a lot of money, so I can't buy my own flat.
If I earned more money, ________________.

c **Complete the text with the correct form of the verbs in brackets.**

What would **you** do if...?

[1] Would you be (you / be) prepared if there was an emergency on your plane?

Think about the last time you flew. Did you pay attention to the safety demonstration? If [2] ________________ (you / not go) to sleep, you would have heard the flight attendant explain the location of the emergency exits. This information is vital. If there had been a fire, [3] ________________ (you / have) only about 90 seconds to get off the plane.

It's unlikely that there will be an emergency on your flight, but if there is, the most important thing is to be ready.

d **Continue the second and third conditional sentences about you.**

1 If my parents were millionaires, ________________.

2 If I could travel anywhere in the world, ________________.

3 If I spoke English fluently, ________________.

4 If I had been born in a different country, ________________.

5 If I had lived in the 19th century, ________________.

6 If I had got up earlier this morning, ________________.

Would you know what to do if [4] ________________ (you / get lost) in the mountains?

The number one survival tip is to stop walking and wait to be rescued. In research done in Canada, however, only two out of 800 lost people actually did this. If [5] ________________ (the others / not keep) walking, rescue services would have found them much more quickly. If they had waited in an open space, [6] ________________ (a helicopter / see) them immediately.

The most important thing when you go hiking is to tell someone where you are going, so that you can be rescued if anything goes wrong.

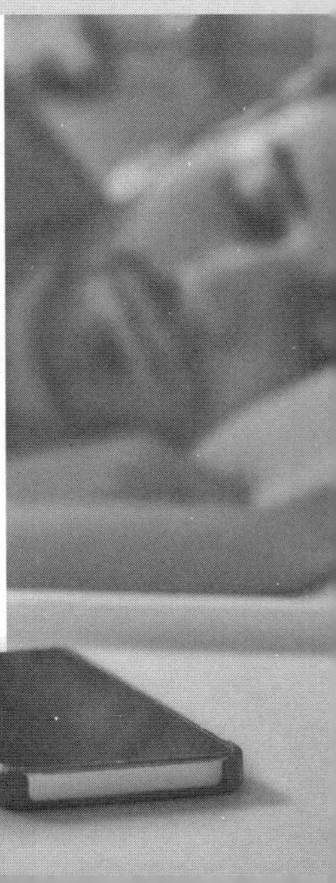

What [7] ________________ (you / do) if you heard somebody in your house in the middle of the night?

Imagine you woke up and there was someone in the kitchen. The worst thing you could do is confront the intruder because he might have a weapon.

Instead you should lock yourself and your family inside a bedroom or the bathroom and call the police. Of course, this would be impossible if [8] ________________ (you / not have) your mobile phone with you. So you should always keep your phone fully charged by the side of your bed.

5B I wish...

G *wish* for the present / future, *wish* for past regrets
V expressing feelings with verbs or *-ed* / *-ing* adjectives
P sentence rhythm and intonation

1 GRAMMAR *wish* for the present / future

a Match 1–8 to a–h.

1 I hardly ever see my partner. d
2 My new clothes are always disappearing. ___
3 The weekend has flown by. ___
4 My brother's playing loud music again. ___
5 I'd love to study abroad. ___
6 The kitchen looks a mess. ___
7 My neighbours' car is always outside my house. ___
8 Public transport is terrible around here. ___

a I wish I had a car.
b I wish he would wear headphones.
c I wish you would do the washing-up.
~~d I wish he didn't work at weekends.~~
e I wish my sister wouldn't borrow them.
f I wish I spoke better English.
g I wish they wouldn't park there.
h I wish it wasn't Monday tomorrow.

b Read the sentences in **a**. Decide if they show that the speaker would like something to be different, or that they are annoyed about something. Complete the chart.

Speaker wants sth to be different	Speaker is annoyed about sth
1	

c Complete the sentences with *wish* + past simple or *wish* + *would*.

1 My friend is driving me mad! He calls me every day.
I wish *my friend wouldn't call me every day*.
2 It's a difficult decision, and I don't know what to do.
I wish *I knew what to do*.
3 My boss really annoys me. She shouts all the time.
I wish ___.
4 I didn't get the job because I can't drive.
I wish ___.
5 I'm fed up with my brother using my computer.
I wish ___.
6 I can't stand it when my son stays in bed all morning.
I wish ___.
7 I want to speak to Dan, but I don't have his phone number.
I wish ___.
8 I hate it when you leave the bathroom in a mess.
I wish ___.
9 I'd love to go away this weekend, but I have to work.
I wish ___.
10 I have lots of books, but I don't have time to read.
I wish ___.

d What would you like to be different? What annoys you? Write six sentences with *wish* + past simple or *wish* + *would*.

1 ___
2 ___
3 ___
4 ___
5 ___
6 ___

2 **VOCABULARY** expressing feelings with verbs or *-ed* / *-ing* adjectives

a Complete the sentences with an adjective or a verb made from the word in brackets.

1 It really *infuriates* me when people talk loudly on their phones on trains. (infuriate)

2 Looking after my sister's three small children is ________________ for my parents. (exhaust)

3 Ethan was so ________________ when he failed his driving test. (disappoint)

4 My girlfriend is scared of flying. The idea of getting on a plane ________________ her. (terrify)

5 My son is a terrible loser. Not winning something really ________________ him. (frustrate)

6 You should try the new Asian restaurant on the high street. The food is ________________. (amaze)

7 I was so ________________ when my phone rang during the meeting. (embarrass)

8 His first visit to the theatre ________________ him to take up acting. (inspire)

9 I find the London Underground quite ________________. I've got on the wrong train several times. (confuse)

10 We were ________________ that so many people came to our party. (thrill)

b Complete the chart.

verb	*-ed* adjective	other adjective
1 delight	*delighted*	*delightful*
2 impress		
3 offend		
4 scare		
5 stress		

c Complete the sentences with the adjectives from **b**.

1 He was *offended* when the teacher suggested he might have cheated in the exam.

2 We were ________________ when we received a surprise visit from some old friends.

3 She gave such an ________________ performance in the film that I think she might win an Oscar.

4 I'm ________________ with your English. You speak really well.

5 The bridge started to move from side to side as we were crossing, which was quite ________________.

6 She's a bit ________________ at the moment because she's looking after her sister's children as well as her own.

7 I found his sexist comments very ________________.

8 Joe's ________________ of small spaces – he never uses the lift.

9 My nieces are ________________ – they're very sweet, and they're always making things for me.

10 My boss is good at staying calm in ________________ situations.

3 VOCABULARY FROM READING

Complete the sentences with a verb or adjective from the list and the prefix *over-* or *under-*.

Verbs

achieve cook ~~flow~~ heat react work

Adjectives

active careful confident emotional qualified

1 Turn the tap off, or the washbasin will *overflow*.

2 If a student begins to ________________ and get bad marks, they should be offered support immediately.

3 Your phone is in the sun – it will ________________.

4 Clara failed the test because she was ________________ about passing and didn't study.

5 They made an effort to ________________ to her comment in order not to cause an argument.

6 My partner can be ________________ with money, so some people think she's tight-fisted.

7 If you ________________ vegetables, they can be too hard to eat.

8 I don't want to work for that company. I've heard that they ________________ their staff.

9 I can't apply for that job. I don't have a degree, so I'm ________________.

10 When we feel depressed, a part of the brain is ________________ and doesn't work as much as it should.

11 We all got ________________ when we had to say goodbye, and everybody started crying.

4 GRAMMAR *wish* for past regrets

a **Match 1–8 to a–h. Then complete a–h with the past perfect form of a verb from the list. Use contractions.**

bring ~~leave~~ not eat not fall not shout
not spend wear work

1 I'm going to be late. e
2 It's colder than I thought today. ____
3 I feel sick. ____
4 I failed half of my exams. ____
5 My leg hurts. ____
6 I've upset my little sister. ____
7 It's pouring with rain. ____
8 I don't have a lot of money left. ____

a I wish I ______________ an umbrella.
b I wish I ______________ so much on that meal last night.
c I wish I ______________ harder.
d I wish I ______________ at her this morning.
~~e I wish I'd left home earlier.~~
f I wish I ______________ off my bike.
g I wish I ______________ a thicker sweater.
h I wish I ______________ that seafood.

b **Read the situation and write sentences beginning with *I wish* + past perfect.**

1 I took the train to work, but it broke down and I was late.
I wish I hadn't taken the train to work.
2 I left my phone on my desk, and now it isn't there.
____
3 I didn't give my boss the report on time, and now she's annoyed with me.
____
4 My girlfriend didn't call me last night, and now I'm worried.
____
5 My friend didn't invite me to her wedding, and now I'm upset.
____
6 We lost our last basketball match, so we won't be playing in the final.
____
7 I was rude to my mother, and now she's offended.
____
8 My son woke me up in the middle of the night, and I couldn't get back to sleep again.
____

5 PRONUNCIATION sentence rhythm and intonation

a **5.2 Listen and complete the sentences.**

1 I wish I'd *applied* for ______________.
2 I wish you'd ______________ at the ______________.
3 I wish I ______________ these ______________.
4 I wish we'd ______________ at ______________.
5 I wish you ______________ me ______________.
6 I wish we ______________ on the ______________.

b **Listen again and repeat the sentences. Copy the rhythm and intonation.**

English File talks to...

Dr Lisa Fenton

Survival expert

1 LOOKING AT LANGUAGE

Complete the common collocations in the sentences.

1 The success of a hike depends on cr*itical* th*ings* ________ like checking the weather before you set off.
2 You'll love this series of documentaries if you're interested in the n________ w________.
3 They say that the Atacama Desert in Chile is a ch________ pl________ to visit.
4 Sunscreen and insect repellent are ess________ it________ if you're going on a safari.
5 It was a r________ pr________ to see turtles laying their eggs on the beach in Mexico.

2 VOCABULARY FROM THE INTERVIEW

Match the words from the interview to the definitions a–h.

1 deadly *f*
2 footwear ____
3 gear ____
4 keep up ____
5 in a bad way ____
6 keep water out ____
7 terrain ____
8 wilderness ____

a equipment
b area of land where it is difficult to live
c stay dry
d land, e.g. rough or flat
e boots or shoes
f ~~poisonous~~
g sick or injured
h move at the same speed as another person

3 THE CONVERSATION

Complete the conversations with the correct topic vocabulary from the list.

a bit of a buzz   potentially risky   ~~risk-averse~~   take risks

1 **A** What would you do if you found yourself in danger?
B I'm a *risk-averse* ________ person, so I wouldn't know.

2 **A** How would you feel about swimming with sharks?
B I think it might be ________, so I wouldn't do it.

3 **A** Why do you think rock climbing appeals to some people?
B I think it gives them ________.

4 **A** What do you think of skiing?
B I don't tend to ________, so I've never tried it.

4 VOCABULARY FROM THE CONVERSATION

Complete the sentences with a word or phrase from the list.

~~being part of something~~   for quite a while
It's not just about you   on a more amateur level   Otherwise

1 We didn't want the expedition to end as we were enjoying *being part of something*.
2 I'd been walking beside the river ________ ________, but I still hadn't found a safe place to cross.
3 One of the guides lent me a hat. ________ ________, my face would have got completely sunburnt.
4 ________ – it's important that everyone in the group feels happy.
5 Even if you go running ________, ________ you should wear the right shoes.

1–5 Can you remember...?

GRAMMAR & VOCABULARY

a Complete the second sentence so that it means the same as the first sentence. Write two to five words. Use the word in brackets.

1 I met John when we were students. (known)
I've known John since ______ we were students.

2 My son's girlfriend is from Hungary; she's young and interesting. (Hungarian)
My son is going out with an ____________ ____________ woman.

3 There's no doubt you'll save money if you sell your car. (certainly)
You ____________ ____________ if you sell your car.

4 It started to rain two hours after we started walking. (had)
We ____________ ____________ two hours when it started to rain.

5 My flight to Amsterdam leaves at 11.00 tomorrow and arrives at 12.15. (flying)
At 12.00 tomorrow, I ____________ ____________ to Amsterdam.

6 My course finishes in May next year. (will)
My course ____________ ____________ by June next year.

7 If the concert isn't sold out, I'll get you a ticket. (unless)
I'll get you a ticket for the concert ____________ ____________.

8 I got a cold because I went out with wet hair. (have)
If I hadn't gone out with wet hair, ____________ ____________ a cold.

9 It annoys me when you don't listen to me. (wish)
I ____________ listen to me.

10 I regret not visiting The Louvre when I was in Paris. (visited)
I ____________ The Louvre when I was in Paris.

b Read the article. Circle a, b, or c.

Thai cave rescue

Boys survive nine days trapped underground

In the summer of 2018, 12 teenage footballers became trapped deep inside a cave in Thailand with the coach who was taking [1]____ them. They had entered the cave to celebrate one of the boy's birthdays, but [2]____ rains had flooded the cave, so they couldn't get out. For nine days, the boys and the coach were sitting in complete darkness, which must have been very [3]____. They managed to survive by drinking the water dripping from the cave walls and by eating the snacks they had bought for the birthday party. The 25-year-old coach, Ekapol Chantawong, wished that he [4]____ with the boys into the cave. [5]____, he refused to eat any of the food so that the boys would have more for themselves. He helped them stay calm by teaching them meditation. When divers [6]____ found the boys, they were [7]____ to see that all the boys were still alive. They were also astonished to find that the boys didn't seem particularly [8]____ by their experience. The rescue team, on the other hand, were in a race against time to get the boys out of the cave before the [9]____ rains began. They had also noticed that the level of oxygen in the cave was dropping. The rescue operation took [10]____ over three days and resulted in all 13 people being taken safely out of the cave.

1	**a** after	**b** care of	**c** pity on
2	**a** hard	**b** heavy	**c** strong
3	**a** scare	**b** scared	**c** scary
4	**a** didn't go	**b** hadn't gone	**c** wouldn't go
5	**a** Apparently	**b** Basically	**c** Certainly
6	**a** eventually	**b** lately	**c** gradually
7	**a** bewildered	**b** grateful	**c** relieved
8	**a** stressed	**b** stress	**c** stressful
9	**a** blizzard	**b** hurricane	**c** monsoon
10	**a** part	**b** place	**c** risks

6A Good night?

G *used to, be used to, get used to*
V sleep
P /s/ and /z/

1 GRAMMAR *used to, be used to, get used to*

a Circle the correct word.

1 Before my sister had children, she used to (*sleep*) / *sleeping* for eight hours every night.
2 When we moved to Britain from Poland, we weren't used to *drive* / *driving* on the left.
3 José got divorced last year, but he soon got used to *live* / *living* on his own.
4 I *used to* / *use to* know her quite well, but we lost touch after university.
5 Max *would* / *used to* have a beard when he was a student.
6 My parents are slowly getting used to *be* / *being* retired.
7 My new job is exhausting. I'm not used to *work* / *working* so hard.
8 Did you use to *play* / *playing* a musical instrument at school?
9 When Lily was a teenager, she *used to* / *was used to* eat pizza almost every day.
10 When I was a child, my dad *would* / *was used to* read to me every night before I went to bed.

b Complete the sentences with the infinitive or gerund of a verb from the list.

be cook go have live look after ~~play~~ study talk use

1 I used to *play* basketball quite well when I was a teenager.
2 Syed is a chef, so he's used to ________ for a lot of people.
3 My sister has got used to ________ in New York now, though she didn't like it at first.
4 My grandparents didn't use to ________ a phone when they were first married.
5 I don't think I could get used to ________ a total vegetarian.
6 When I was a child, my whole family would ________ for a walk every Sunday afternoon.
7 Grace has never lived on her own before, so she isn't used to ________ herself.
8 Did you use to ________ with music on when you were at university?
9 Ben will have to get used to ________ public transport when he starts his new job.
10 People used to ________ to friends in person, not online.

c Complete the second sentence so that it has a similar meaning to the first sentence. Use a form of *used to*, *be used to*, or *get used to* and a verb.

1 Stephen wasn't so affectionate in the past.
Stephen *didn't use to be* so affectionate.
2 Has working at night become less of a problem now?
Have you ________ at night?
3 Rob couldn't sleep because he doesn't normally sleep on a sofa.
Rob couldn't sleep because he ________ on a sofa.
4 Chloe wore her sister's clothes when she was a child.
Chloe ________ her sister's clothes when she was a child.
5 We have adapted to living in the country very quickly.
We have ________ in the country very quickly.
6 In the past, the high street was full of shops, but now many have closed down.
The high street ________ full of shops, but now many have closed down.
7 They still don't know how to use the new computer system – they keep making mistakes.
They haven't ________ the new computer system yet.
8 I don't normally have breakfast so early.
I'm ________ breakfast so early.

d Write about things you *used to* / *didn't use to* do as a child and things you're *used to* / *you've got used to* doing these days.

When I was a child...

____

____

____

____

____

____

____

____

These days...

____

____

____

____

____

____

____

____

2 PRONUNCIATION /s/ and /z/

a 6.1 Listen and complete the sentences.

1 Terry is <u>used to working</u> at night.
2 We've got __________ in a tiny flat.
3 Antibiotics are drugs that are __________ infections.
4 I never __________ problems sleeping.
5 I __________ a room, but now I have my own.
6 A trolley is a small vehicle that is __________ things.

b Listen again. In which sentences is *used* pronounced /juːzd/ and in which is it pronounced /juːst/?

c Listen again and repeat the sentences. <u>Co</u>py the <u>rhy</u>thm.

d Write the words in the correct column.

~~bus~~ ~~buzz~~ cause course eyes ice loose lose peace peas place plays price prize race raise

 1 **snake**	 2 **zebra**
bus	buzz

e 6.2 Listen and check. Then listen again and repeat the words.

3 VOCABULARY sleep

a Complete the sentences.

1 It's very hot in the summer where we live, so we only have a sh*eet*________ on the bed.
2 We were cold in bed, so we got a bl__________ from the cupboard.
3 She has to wear earplugs at night because her husband sn__________.
4 I was feeling sl__________, so I went to bed.
5 My grandmother takes sl__________ p__________ to help her to sleep.
6 If I get up early, I try to have a n__________ after lunch.
7 It was lovely and warm in the bed because there was a nice thick d__________ on it.
8 I was so tired that I fell asleep as soon as I put my head on the p__________.
9 James has in__________ – he just can't sleep at night.
10 I tried not to y__________, but I was tired and I couldn't help it.

b Match 1–6 to a–f.

1 I didn't hear last night's storm – I always sleep *e*
2 Before I travel, I often have ____
3 Our children were ____
4 Apparently, I used to sleepwalk when I was a child; ____
5 I often fall ____
6 If you oversleep, ____

a nightmares about missing my flight.
b fast asleep by the time we got home.
c you'll miss your bus.
d asleep during long coach journeys.
~~e like a log.~~
f one day my mother found me in the garden!

c Complete the questions with the correct form of a verb from the list.

be fall feel have oversleep ~~sleep~~ sleepwalk snore

1 How often do you *sleep*________ like a log? Why?
2 Do you ever __________ nightmares? What about?
3 When was the last time you __________? What time did you wake up?
4 How long does it usually take you to __________ asleep?
5 Do you know anyone who __________? If so, where do they usually go?
6 When was the last time you __________ fast asleep and something or someone woke you up?
7 What makes you __________ sleepy? Why?
8 Do you know anyone who __________? How much noise do they make?

d Answer the questions in c about you.

1 __________
2 __________
3 __________
4 __________
5 __________
6 __________
7 __________
8 __________

6B Music and emotion

G gerunds and infinitives
V music; words from other languages
P words from other languages

1 GRAMMAR gerunds and infinitives

a Circle a, b, or c.

1 Mia learned ____ the guitar when she was a teenager.
a play **b** to play **c** playing

2 I don't mind ____ if you tell me which way to go.
a drive **b** to drive **c** driving

3 I must ____ to some of their songs before I go to the concert.
a listen **b** to listen **c** listening

4 Our teacher makes us ____ a lot of homework.
a do **b** to do **c** doing

5 Alvaro's doctor suggested ____ a specialist about his back.
a see **b** to see **c** seeing

6 We'd like ____ our bill now as we're leaving before breakfast tomorrow.
a pay **b** to pay **c** paying

7 I start work early in the morning, so I don't like ____ on weekdays.
a go out **b** to go out **c** going out

8 The man denied ____ the laptop from my bag.
a steal **b** to steal **c** stealing

9 Kim expects ____ her exam results on Friday.
a get **b** to get **c** getting

10 I've given up ____ to the gym. It was too boring.
a go **b** to go **c** going

11 I can't imagine ____ at 5.30 every morning.
a get up **b** to get up **c** getting up

12 My son managed ____ his driving test although he was really nervous.
a pass **b** to pass **c** passing

b **Complete the sentences with the infinitive or gerund of the verb in brackets.**

1 I remembered *to buy* ________ milk, but I didn't get any bread! (buy)

2 If you can't sleep at night, try ________ for a while. (read)

3 My sister is trying ________ a new job – she doesn't get on with her boss. (find)

4 We need ________ a plumber because the shower's broken. (call)

5 That shirt needs ________ if you want to wear it tonight. (iron)

6 Laura forgot ________ her mother a birthday card. (send)

7 I'll never forget ________ my best friend for the first time. (meet)

8 I remember ________ the apple tree when I was a child. (climb)

c **Complete the questions with the infinitive or gerund of a verb from the list.**

add buy ~~download~~ go learn
listen to see want

1 What's the first song or album you remember downloading ______?
2 Which song always makes you ______ to dance?
3 Which artist or band would you most like ______ in concert?
4 Have you ever tried ______ an instrument? Which one?
5 Are there any songs you like at the moment that need ______ to your playlist?
6 What kind of music do you avoid ______ if you can?
7 Have you ever forgotten ______ tickets for a concert, and then it sold out? Which concert?
8 Would you rather ______ to a small concert or a large music festival? Why?

d **Answer the questions in c about you.**

1 ______
2 ______
3 ______
4 ______
5 ______
6 ______
7 ______
8 ______

2 VOCABULARY & PRONUNCIATION
music; words from other languages

a **Complete the missing letters.**

1 s_o_p_r_a_no

2 s__x__ph________

3 b______ g____t____

4 ch______

5 fl______

6 v____l____

7 k____b________

8 c__l____

9 dr______

10 o__ch____t____

b **Match the English words borrowed from other languages to the definitions.**

~~ballet~~ chorus concerto encore genre mezzo-soprano rhythm symphony

1 a style of dancing that tells a story with music but without words ballet
2 a long piece of music for a large orchestra, usually in three or four parts ________
3 a short, extra performance at the end of a concert ________
4 a singing voice with a range between soprano and alto ________
5 part of a song that is sung after each verse ________
6 a strong, regular, repeated pattern of sounds ________
7 a piece of music for an orchestra and one instrument playing a solo ________
8 a particular type or style of e.g. music ________

c **Underline the stressed syllable in the words in the list. Then put them in the correct column.**

~~bal|let~~ cel|lo cho|rus con|cer|to con|duc|tor en|core gen|re gui|tar key|board or|ches|tra rhy|thm sax|o|phone so|pra|no sym|pho|ny vi|o|lin

Stress on first syllable	Stress on second syllable	Stress on third syllable
ballet		

d **6.3 Listen and check. Then listen again and repeat the words.**

e **Circle the word with a different sound.**

keys	1 **ch**ill **ch**oir or**ch**estra psy**ch**ic
chess	2 ar**ch**itect **c**ello **c**iao con**c**erto
shower	3 **ch**ampagne **ch**auffeur **ch**ef **ch**orus

f **6.4 Listen and check. Then listen again and repeat the words.**

g **6.5 Listen and complete the sentences.**

1 The barista was the first to find the graffiti.
2 The r________ picked them up after the ________.
3 A lot of ________ took ________ of the film star.
4 The technician gave the ________ a ________.
5 The dancers in that ________ had a natural sense of ________.

h **Listen again and repeat the sentences. Copy the rhythm.**

7A You be the judge

G past modals: *must have*, etc.; *would rather*
V verbs often confused
P weak form of *have*

1 GRAMMAR past modals: *must have*, etc.

a Match the sentences to the responses.

1 Ryan's phone was switched off. c
2 Stacey can't find her gloves. ___
3 Emma didn't make her bed this morning. ___
4 I was surprised that Darius didn't come to the party. ___
5 Leo has just bought a brand new Porsche. ___
6 Isabel didn't say hello to me this morning. ___
7 I'm not sure where Millie is. ___
8 My dad was made redundant when we were kids. ___

a She can't have seen you.
b She may have left them in her car.
~~c I think he might have been at the cinema.~~
d He must have paid a fortune for it.
e She could have gone to a friend's house.
f She might not have had time.
g He couldn't have been very happy about that.
h He must have had something else to do.

b Complete the sentences with *must have*, *might have*, *might not have*, or *can't have* and the verb in brackets.

1 You must have been delighted when you passed your driving test – it was your first time, wasn't it? (be)
2 I'm not sure where Ali is, but he ______________ home. He wasn't feeling well this morning. (go)
3 You ______________ my parents at the supermarket. They're away on holiday. (see)
4 I don't know why my grandmother didn't open the door, but I suppose she ______________ the bell. (hear)
5 The 'For Sale' sign is still up outside their house. They ______________ yet. (move)
6 I don't understand how the accident happened, but the driver ______________ asleep. (fall)
7 Those boys look really guilty. They ______________ something wrong. (do)
8 Erika hasn't replied to my email. It's possible that she ______________ it yet. (read)

c Write the next sentence using the words given.

1 My brother isn't talking to me.
I / should / shout at him
I shouldn't have shouted at him.

2 We're running out of petrol.
we / should / fill up at the last petrol station
____

3 Someone has taken Ben's phone.
he / ought / leave it on his desk
____

4 You won't be able to walk in those shoes.
you / should / buy such high heels
____

5 I had a nightmare last night.
I / ought / stay up to watch that horror film
____

6 Your cousins look really scruffy.
they / ought / dress up for the wedding
____

7 My alarm clock isn't working.
it / should / go off at 7.30
____

8 Jessie missed her train.
she / should / take a taxi to the station
____

d Look at the photo. What do you think happened? What do you think the cyclist did wrong? Use *must*, *might* / *may* / *could*, or *can't* / *couldn't* to make deductions, and *should have* / *ought to have* to express criticism. Use the words in the list or your own ideas.

be / more careful   break / bike   ~~fall off / bike~~   hit / head   hurt / leg   ride / so fast   sprain / ankle   wear / protection

1 She must have fallen off her bike.
2 ______
3 ______
4 ______
5 ______
6 ______
7 ______
8 ______

2 PRONUNCIATION weak form of *have*

a 7.1 Listen and write the sentences with either *have* or *of*.

1 I cried at the end of the film.
2 ______
3 ______
4 ______
5 ______
6 ______

b Listen again and repeat the sentences. Copy the rhythm.

c 7.2 Listen and complete the sentences.

1 They're taking Steve to hospital. He might have broken a bone.
2 Leyla isn't here yet. She can't have ______ my ______.
3 It was only a joke. She shouldn't have ______ so ______.
4 This restaurant's packed. We should have ______ a ______.
5 I didn't hear the phone. I must have ______.
6 Becky and Ian haven't come to the party. They may have ______ about it.

d Listen again and repeat the second sentences. Copy the rhythm.

3 GRAMMAR IN CONTEXT *would rather*

Rewrite the sentences using *would rather.*

1 I'd prefer it if you didn't post photos of me on social media.
I'd rather you didn't post photos of me on social media.
2 I don't really want to cook tonight, if you don't mind.
I ______.
3 Would you prefer to stay in or go out?
What ______?
4 I'd prefer it if we got a taxi home, if that's OK with you.
I ______.
5 I'd prefer to see that film at the cinema than on TV.
I ______.
6 I'd prefer to sit by the window than next to the aisle.
I ______.

4 **VOCABULARY** verbs often confused

a Complete the sentences with the correct **bold** verb.

1 **wish** / **hope**
I wish ________ we had enough money to buy a bigger flat.

2 **mind** / **matter**
I don't ____________ where we go. The important thing is to have a holiday.

3 **avoid** / **prevent**
My daughter will do anything to ____________ doing housework. She's really lazy.

4 **remember** / **remind**
____________ me to send my dad a card. It's his birthday next week.

5 **argue** / **discuss**
My boyfriend and I often ____________ about his friends. I really don't like them.

6 **lend** / **borrow**
Could I ____________ your phone charger? I've left mine at home.

7 **notice** / **realize**
I didn't ____________ what the thief was wearing. It was too dark.

8 **beat** / **win**
Chelsea managed to ____________ the match 1–0.

9 **expect** / **wait**
I'll ____________ outside while you see the doctor.

10 **raise** / **rise**
Please ____________ your hand if you have any questions.

11 **advise** / **warn**
My uncle asked me to ____________ him which laptop he should get.

12 **deny** / **refuse**
I ____________ to lend Harry any more money. He never pays me back!

13 **lay** / **lie**
All I want to do when I'm on holiday is ____________ on the beach and sunbathe.

14 **rob** / **steal**
Don't leave your phone on the table – somebody might ____________ it.

b Complete the sentences with the past simple form of a verb from the pairs in the list.

advise / warn argue / discuss avoid / prevent
beat / win deny / refuse expect / wait lay / lie
lend / borrow mind / matter notice / realize raise / rise
~~remember / remind~~ rob / steal wish / hope

1 When I got to my car, I suddenly remembered that the keys were in my other bag.
2 My parents ________________ me the money to buy a new computer, but I have to pay them back
3 Scotland ________________ Ireland 3–2.
4 Two people ________________ me while I was walking home. They got away with my purse and phone.
5 My colleague ________________ taking my scissors, but I saw them later on his desk.
6 Last year, we just ________________ on the beach all day when we were on holiday.
7 House prices ________________ last month for the first time this year.
8 At the meeting we ________________ the possibility of working together.
9 The police officer's action ________________ anybody from getting hurt.
10 I ________________ our team to lose, but in the end they won.
11 He didn't think it ________________ that his wife travelled a lot because he had a busy job, too.
12 The moment I heard her voice on the phone, I ________________ something was wrong.
13 The tour guide ________________ us that the area was dangerous at night.
14 We ________________ the weather would be good for the picnic, but unfortunately it rained.

7B Only an act

G verbs of the senses
V the body
P silent consonants

1 GRAMMAR verbs of the senses

a Circle the correct form.

1. Your skin *feels* / *feels like* dry. You need to use some cream.
2. Ken is sweating. He *looks* / *looks as if* he's been running.
3. We need to take out the rubbish. The kitchen *smells* / *smells like* terrible.
4. I'm not sure what's in this curry, but it *tastes like* / *tastes as if* chicken.
5. It *sounds* / *sounds as though* Becky has finally got up. I can hear her moving around.
6. Come in and sit by the fire. Your hands *feel like* / *feel as if* ice!
7. This soup *tastes* / *tastes as if* you put a lot of garlic in it.
8. You *seem* / *seem like* happy today. Have you had some good news?
9. I don't feel like *go* / *going out* tonight. Let's stay in and watch a film.
10. You *sound* / *sound like* your mother when you talk like that.

b Complete the sentences with *look* / *feel* / *smell* / *sound* / *taste* / *seem* + *like* or *as if* where necessary.

1. My skin feels ______ much softer since I've been using a new face cream.
2. What's that noise? It ______ thunder.
3. Ellen's boyfriend ______ a model – he's tall and incredibly good-looking.
4. Have you turned off the cooker? It ______ something's burning.
5. This salad ______ horrible – it's really salty.
6. This swimming pool ______ it's heated. The water is lovely and warm!
7. Your voice ______ strange. Do you have a sore throat?
8. Is anything the matter? You ______ a bit distant today.
9. That aftershave ______ petrol – I'm not sure if I like it.
10. Martha's hair is in a mess. She ______ she's just got out of bed.

c Complete the description of the thing in photo 1 with *looks*, *smells*, *feels*, or *tastes*. Then write descriptions of the things in photos 2–4 using verbs of the senses.

1 a cake

2 garlic

3 blue cheese

4 a Siamese cat

1 It's a kind of food. It looks ______ a bit like bread. It ______ hot and quite soft at first, but it goes harder on the outside when it's cold. It ______ delicious when it comes out of the oven, and it ______ even better when you eat it.

2 ______________________________

3 ______________________________

4 ______________________________

2 **VOCABULARY** the body

a Complete the missing letters.

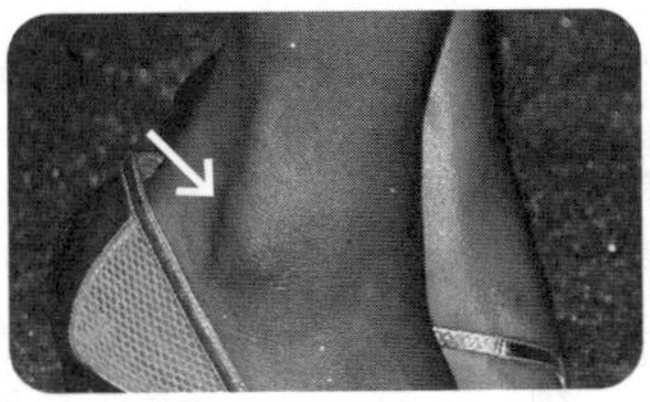

1 a_n_k_l_e_

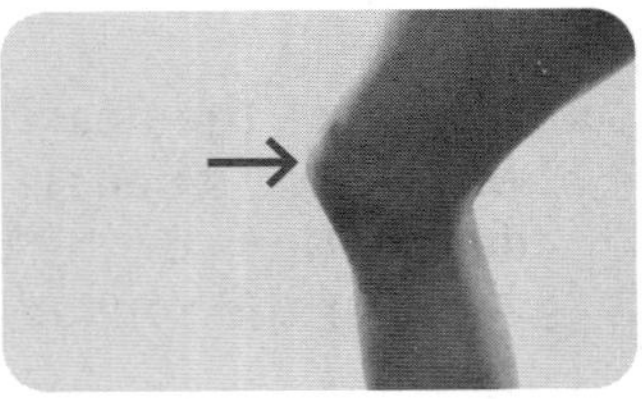

2 kn___ ___

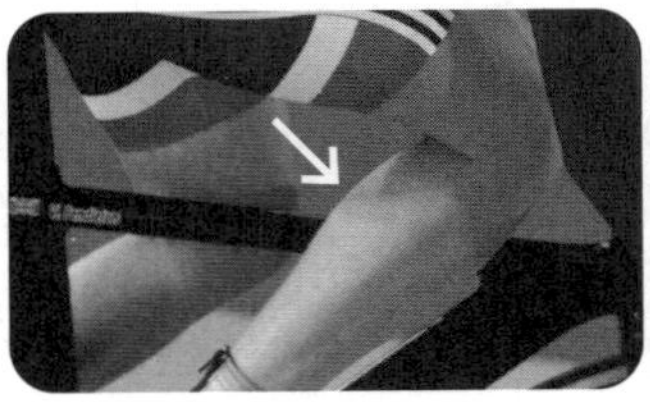

3 c___ ___ ___

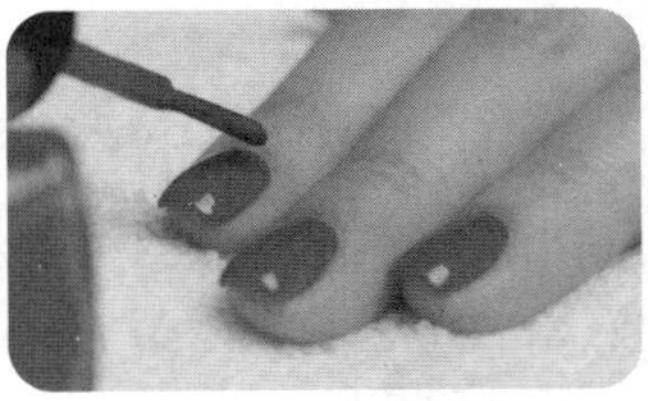

4 n___ ___ ___s

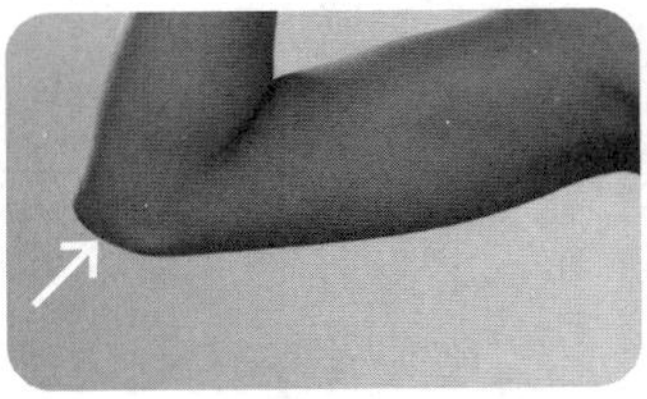

5 e___b___ ___

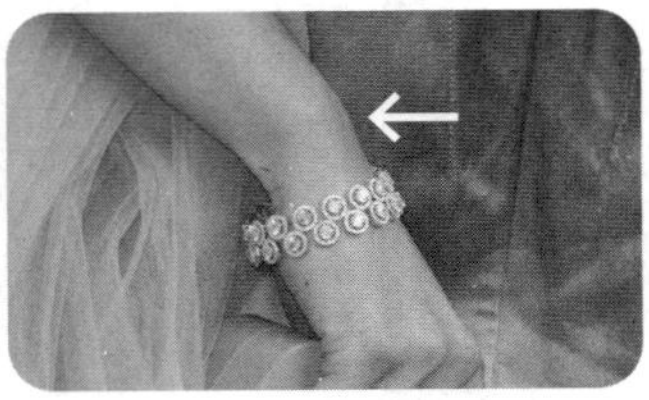

6 wr___ ___ ___

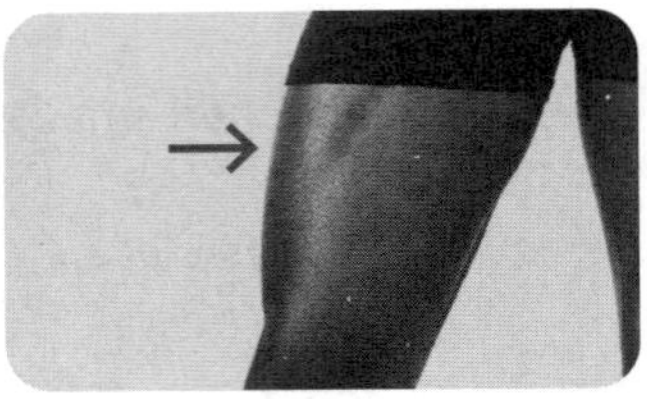

7 th___ ___ ___

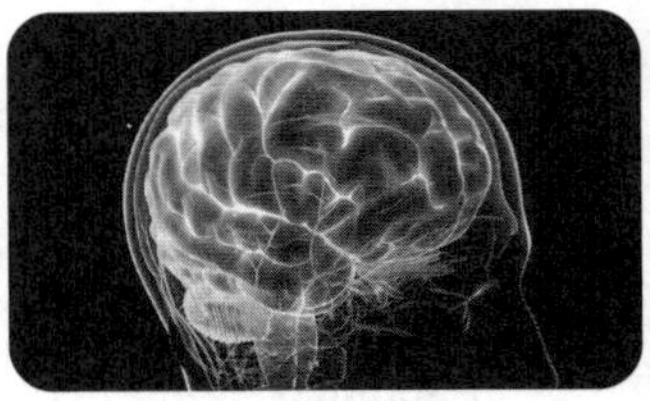

8 br___ ___ ___

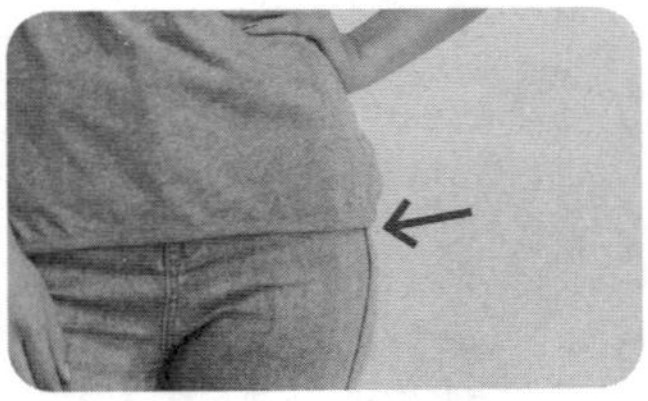

9 h___ ___

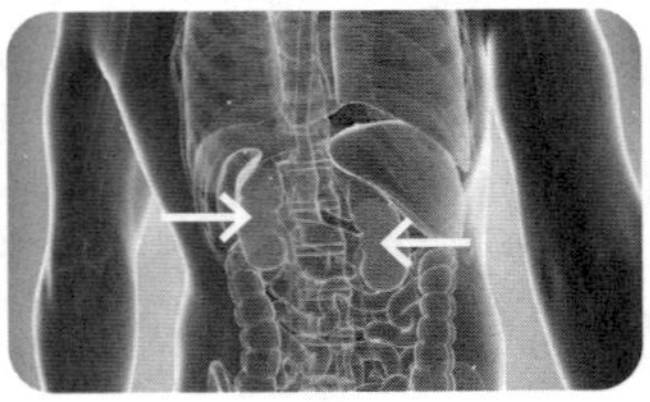

10 k___ ___n___ ___s

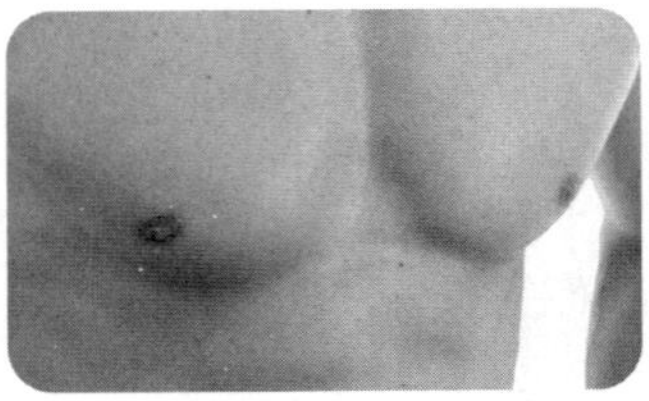

11 ch___ ___ ___

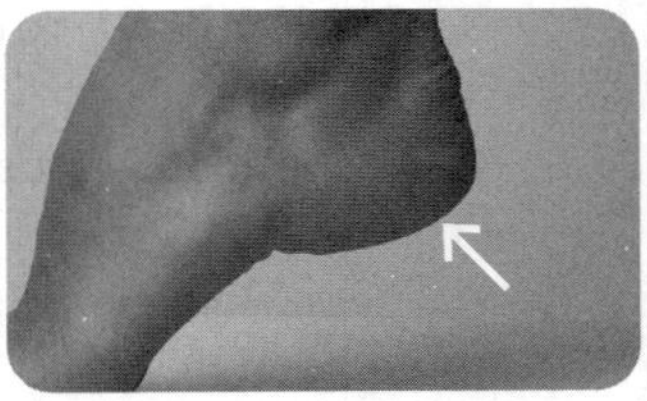

12 h___ ___ ___

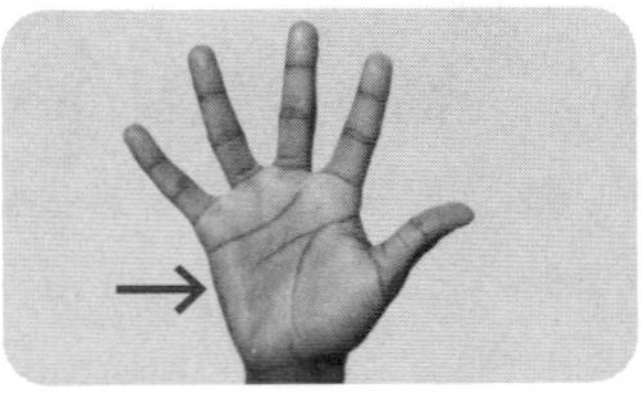

13 p___ ___ ___

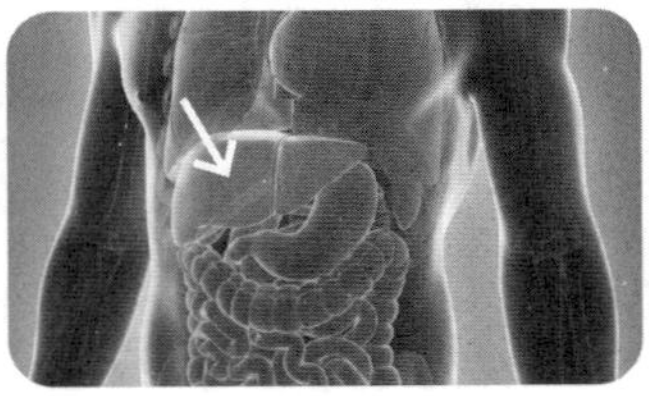

14 l___v___ ___

15 w___ ___ ___t

16 b___t___ ___ ___

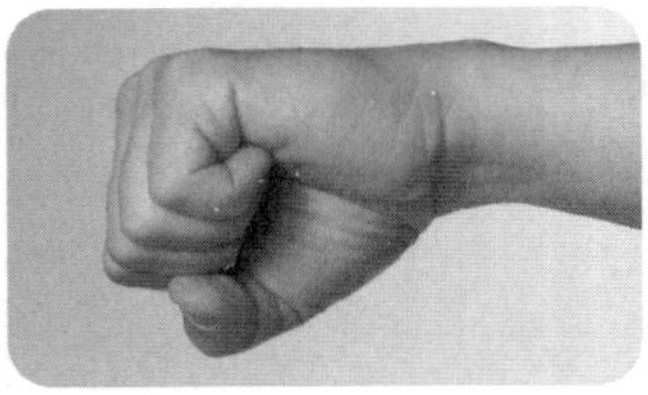

17 f___ ___ ___

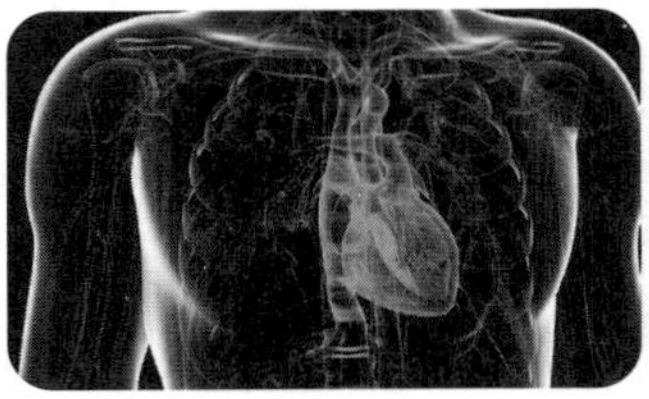

18 h___ ___ ___t

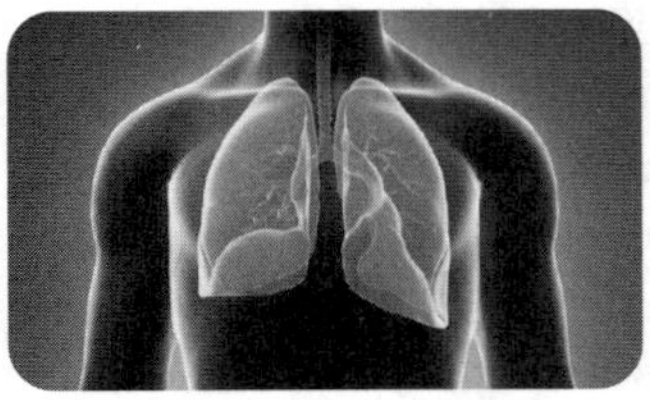

19 l___ ___ ___s

b Match 1–13 to a–m.

1 Can you touch _h_
2 When I asked if she'd passed, she shook ___
3 I always brush ___
4 Adam shrugged ___
5 Here's a tissue so you can blow ___
6 I used to suck ___
7 Jessie combed ___
8 She went into the room and shook ___
9 Remember to brush ___
10 When I told my boss, she raised ___
11 My boyfriend bites ___
12 He folded ___
13 My niece held ___

a your nose.
b my hand as we walked down the road.
c her head sadly.
d his arms and stood watching me.
e my thumb when I was a baby.
f his nails when he's nervous.
g her hair and put on her jacket to go out.
~~h your toes?~~
i his shoulders and said he didn't know.
j your hair once you've washed it.
k hands with the interviewer.
l her eyebrows in surprise.
m my teeth after every meal.

c **Match the verbs in the list to the parts of the body they are related to.**

~~chew~~ frown hug kneel point scratch
stare stretch wave wink yawn

1 knees ________
2 hand ________
3 eye(s) ________ ________
4 finger ________
5 mouth *chew* ________
6 arms ________ ________
7 nails ________
8 forehead ________

d **Complete the sentences with the past simple form of the verbs in c.**

1 The children *stared* at the ice cream in the shop window.
2 Anna ________ her son and gave him a kiss before she left the house.
3 He ________ as he read the letter – it can't have been good news.
4 We ________ each mouthful to make it last because we didn't know when we'd be eating again.
5 He got up and ________ to try and wake himself up.
6 The police officer ________ on the ground to examine the footprints.
7 I don't speak French, so I just ________ at the cake I wanted.
8 My friend ________ at me when he saw me getting off the train.
9 My dad ________ at my daughter to show he wasn't being serious.
10 The baby ________ twice and then fell asleep.
11 Robin ________ the insect bites on his legs and made them bleed.

3 PRONUNCIATION silent consonants

a **~~Cross out~~ the silent consonants in the words. Use the phonetics to help you.**

1 ~~w~~rist /rɪst/
2 thumb /θʌm/
3 kneel /niːl/
4 palm /pɑːm/
5 muscle /ˈmʌsl/
6 whistle /ˈwɪsl/
7 honest /ˈɒnɪst/
8 fasten /ˈfɑːsn/
9 aisle /aɪl/
10 design /dɪˈzaɪn/
11 whole /həʊl/

b **7.3 Listen and check. Then listen again and repeat the words.**

c **Look at the phonetics. Write the word.**

1 /ˈkɑːsl/ *castle*
2 /huːz/ ________
3 /ˈkʌbəd/ ________
4 /ˈfɒrən/ ________
5 /rɒŋ/ ________
6 /kɑːm/ ________
7 /naɪf/ ________
8 /ˈsɪzəz/ ________
9 /ˈɔːtəm/ ________
10 /ˈaɪlənd/ ________
11 /wɒt/ ________
12 /ˈplʌmə(r)/ ________

d **7.4 Listen and check. Then listen again and repeat the words.**

e **7.5 Listen and complete the sentences.**

1 They spent the *whole* meeting discussing the new project.
2 I wish I had been more ________ about how I felt.
3 I don't know anyone who likes the ________ of the new shopping centre.
4 It seems to have been much colder than usual this ________.
5 I've found a key, but I don't know ________ it is.
6 She looked surprisingly ________ after the accident.

4 COLLOQUIAL ENGLISH

English File talks to...

Benedict Cumberbatch

Actor

1 LOOKING AT LANGUAGE

Complete the sophisticated language in the sentences.

1. Everyone in my family played a music instrument, so **it was n**ormalized____ **very early on**.
2. When it comes to good cooks, my grandmother is the first person **that springs to m**__________.
3. There was a positive atmosphere in the class – everyone seemed **e**__________ **to** learn.
4. As a child, I was **very w**__________ of using the lift in our apartment block – it was always breaking down.
5. My languages **stood me in good st**__________ when it came to finding a job.
6. I never failed an exam at school, so I did well **in that r**__________.

2 VOCABULARY FROM THE INTERVIEW

Complete the sentences with a word or phrase from the list.

adaptation   audition   ~~empathy~~
hang me out to dry   have a good ear
mind was blown wide open   prove yourself
rehearsals

1. Both authors have the skill to make you feel empathy__________ with their characters.
2. I hope they won't __________________ because of one silly mistake.
3. There are only three __________________ left before the opening night of the play.
4. The new screen __________________ of Shakespeare's *Macbeth* is excellent.
5. You need to __________________ to play the piano really well.
6. The experience was incredible. My __________________.
7. You have to __________________ in your first role if you want to be given bigger parts in the future.
8. She had an __________________ for a part in *The Rings of Power*.

3 THE CONVERSATION

Complete the conversations with a discourse marker from the list.

Also   ~~For instance~~   However   Probably

1 **A** A good film can bring out that complexity of a certain part of a person's life.
B Yeah.
A For instance, *Oppenheimer*.

2 **A** My kids are now big fans of Queen.
B Really?
A __________ mainly because of the film, *Bohemian Rhapsody*.

3 **A** I don't think a biopic can teach you everything about a person.
B No.
A __________, I think it's a good way of learning about aspects of a person's life.

4 **A** A biopic can change your opinion about someone famous.
B That's right.
A __________, a biopic can tell you about someone you don't know anything about.

4 VOCABULARY FROM THE CONVERSATION

Complete the sentences with a phrase from the list.

black and white   in short   ~~puts on~~   so wrong   to life

1. And she puts on__________ her own concert in Carnegie Hall.
2. I think, __________________, no. Not really.
3. I thought it was a very __________________ thing.
4. ...the film sort of brought those dilemmas __________________ for me.
5. I thought they got his personality __________________.

1-7 Can you remember...?

GRAMMAR & VOCABULARY

a Complete the sentences with the correct form of the **bold** word.

1 My sister-in-law is rather ____________-____________. She has a very high opinion of herself. **HEAD**

2 The boys were wearing ____________ tops, so you couldn't see their faces. **HOOD**

3 ____________, there's nothing we can do about the current situation; it's up to the politicians. **BASIC**

4 They've said the weather will be ____________, so take an umbrella in case it rains later. **CHANGE**

5 Toby's moving house at the moment, which is a bit ____________. **STRESS**

6 The town hall is an ____________ building in the main square. **IMPRESS**

7 I ____________ this morning, so I was late for work. **SLEEP**

8 She gets really ____________ when she can't play the piece she's practising on her flute. **FRUSTRATE**

9 I ____________ in bed for hours last night trying to get to sleep. **LIE**

10 Mirga is a famous ____________ who has worked with orchestras all over the world. **CONDUCT**

b Read the article. Circle a, b, or c.

So you want to be an actor?

Many people think that acting [1] easy. That might be because, on a surface level, the only thing actors need to do is remember their lines and say them to the camera. People say, 'I [2] be an actor, if I could memorize words easily.' However, nobody would expect to become a professional singer overnight. In general, most people think that becoming a [3] requires far more training than appearing on-screen.

In fact, it takes just as much training to be a good actor [4] it does to become an opera singer. The difference is that an actor has to learn [5] naturally so that the audience doesn't [6] that he or she is acting. According to the famous teacher Stanford Meisner, 'Acting is behaving truthfully under imaginary circumstances.'

If a person [7] to become a successful actor, they have to learn how to bring a script to life. From the moment he or she receives the pages, an actor will [8] for action in the lines in order to make choices about his or her performance. It's true that the writer wrote the words, but it's the actor who creates a believable character to express them.

In conclusion, it is impossible to decide spontaneously one day to go and get an acting job. The naturalness of an actor's performance might make you [9] that anyone who can read or speak can be one. However, it's more than likely that it [10] them many years of training to get where they are now.

	a	b	c
1	**a** looks	**b** looks like	**c** looks as if
2	**a** can	**b** could	**c** will be able to
3	**a** concerto	**b** soprano	**c** symphony
4	**a** as	**b** like	**c** than
5	**a** perform	**b** performing	**c** to perform
6	**a** advise	**b** deny	**c** realize
7	**a** had wanted	**b** wanted	**c** wants
8	**a** be looking	**b** have looked	**c** to look
9	**a** think	**b** thinking	**c** to think
10	**a** had taken	**b** has been taking	**c** has taken

8A Modern crime

G the passive (all forms); *have something done*; *it is said that…*, *he is thought to…*, etc.
V crime and punishment
P the letter *u*

1 VOCABULARY crime and punishment

a Complete the text with the words in the list.

~~be burgled~~ break into burglars burglary steal

I never thought that my flat would [1] *be burgled* because I live on the third floor. But one day, I came home to find the lock on my front door was broken. When I called the police to report the [2] __________, a police officer came to the flat and had a look round. She said that the [3] __________ had probably climbed over the roofs of the houses behind to [4] __________ the flat through a window. They had then broken the lock on the front door to leave. The thieves didn't [5] __________ much – just some money and an old camera of mine – but I was shocked that it had been so easy for them to get into my flat.

b Read the definitions and complete the missing letters in the crime.

1 entering a building illegally and stealing things from it
b *u* *r* gl *a* *r* *y*

2 killing somebody deliberately
m__ __d__ __

3 giving money or valuable items to a person to persuade them to help you
br__b__ __ __

4 following and watching somebody over a long period of time, in a way that is annoying or frightening
st__ __k__ __ __

5 destroying or damaging something, especially public property, deliberately and for no good reason
v__ __d__l__ __ __

6 demanding money from a person by threatening to tell somebody else a secret about them
bl__ __ __m__ __ __

7 using violence or threats to take control of a vehicle, often in order to demand something from a government
h__j__ck__ __ __

8 dealing illegal drugs
dr__ __ d__ __l__ __ __

9 using violent action in order to achieve political aims or force a government to act
t__rr__r__ __ __

10 finding a way to look at or change information on somebody else's computer system without permission
h__ck__ __ __

11 stealing something from a person or place
th__ __ __

12 cheating somebody to get money or goods illegally
fr__ __ __

13 stealing money from a bank, shop, person, etc., especially using violence or threats
r__bb__ __ __

14 attacking somebody violently in order to steal their money, especially in a public place
m__gg__ __ __

15 taking, sending, or bringing goods secretly or illegally into or out of a country
sm__ __ __l__ __ __

16 taking somebody away illegally and keeping them as a prisoner, especially in order to get money
k__ __n__pp__ __ __

c **Complete the chart.**

Criminal	Verb
[1] *burglar*	burgle
[2]	murder
✗	bribe
[3]	stalk
[4]	vandalize
[5]	blackmail
[6]	hijack
[7]	deal drugs
[8]	hack
[9]	rape
[10]	steal
[11]	commit fraud
[12]	rob
[13]	mug
[14]	smuggle
[15]	kidnap

d **Complete the sentences with the past simple form of a verb from c.**

1 Police are looking for a man who attacked and *raped* __________ a woman yesterday afternoon.

2 Fortunately, the gang __________ the bank when there were no customers inside.

3 The woman __________ the actor for many years, following him wherever he went.

4 They __________ $1 million worth of electronic goods into the country before they were caught at customs.

5 The construction company __________ the mayor with tens of thousands of pounds for permission to build houses on the land.

6 Two men __________ my friend at knifepoint yesterday. They took all her money.

7 The woman __________ fraud by pretending she was a psychic and charging people.

8 Some people __________ my house while I was away and took all my music equipment.

9 They __________ the man by shooting him dead in the street.

10 Someone __________ my car from outside my house last night.

11 They __________ the man by threatening to send the photographs to his wife if he didn't pay them the money.

12 Two armed men __________ the plane and forced the pilot to take them to the nearest airport.

13 The boy __________ drugs because he thought it was an easier way to get money than having a job.

14 A couple __________ the politician as he left his house and later demanded £1 million for his safe return.

15 Youths __________ the park last night and damaged a lot of trees and flowers.

16 Someone __________ my computer last month and stole my personal details.

e **Complete the text with the words in the lists.**

Nouns

court evidence judge jury proof punishment verdict witnesses

Verbs

accused acquitted arrest catch charged committed ~~investigate~~ question sentenced

It is the job of the police to [1] *investigate* __________ crimes and try to [2] __________ the criminal or criminals who [3] __________ the crime. When the police have a suspect, they can [4] __________ him or her and take them to the police station to [5] __________ them. If the suspect is [6] __________ with the crime, they have to appear in front of a [7] __________ and maybe a [8] __________ (of 12 people) in [9] __________. Here they are [10] __________ of the crime and [11] __________ may be called to give [12] __________. If there is no [13] __________ that they were involved in the crime, they are [14] __________. If not, they have to wait for the [15] __________. If they are found guilty, they are given a [16] __________. In some cases, they may be [17] __________ to spend a period of time in prison.

2 PRONUNCIATION the letter *u*

a Circle the word with a different sound.

bird	1 burglar murderer verdict very
up	2 community drugs judge smuggle
tourist	3 during future jury secure
/juː/	4 accuse new punish useful
horse	5 court guilty stalker fraud

b 8.1 Listen and check. Then listen again and repeat the words.

3 GRAMMAR the passive (all forms); *have something done*; *it is said that...*, *he is thought to...*, etc.

a Complete the text with the correct active or passive form of the verbs in brackets.

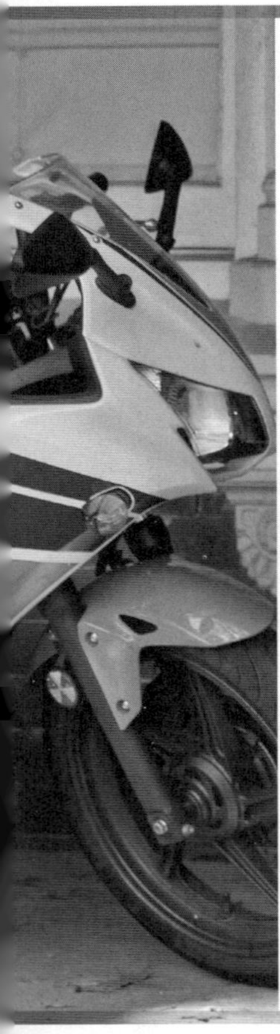

Last month, my motorbike [1] was taken (take) from outside my house. When I called the police, I [2] found out (find out) that over 20 motorbikes [3] ________ (steal) in my area in the previous six months. The officer I spoke to promised me that the thief would [4] ________ (catch) as soon as possible.

First, the police [5] ________ (question) all the victims of the thefts and [6] ________ (visit) all the motorbike dealers in the area. Their investigations came to an end late last night when they identified the criminal...as my next-door neighbour!

He [7] ________ (just arrest), and at the moment he [8] ________ (hold) at the local police station. His case [9] ________ (hear) in the magistrate's court next week and everyone [10] ________ (expect) him to be found guilty. He might [11] ________ (give) a short prison sentence, but the best thing is that no more motorbikes [12] ________ (steal) in my area in the future.

b Rewrite the sentences with *have something done*.

1 Someone is going to change the lock on my front door.
I'm going to have the lock on my front door changed.

2 Someone tests our burglar alarm twice a year.
We ________ twice a year.

3 A mechanic has repaired my car.
I ________.

4 Someone broke our windows when we were on holiday.
We ________ when we were on holiday.

5 Someone will clean my carpets in the spring.
I ________ in the spring.

6 Someone has hacked my boyfriend's computer.
My boyfriend ________.

7 Someone cleans Oliver's flat once a week.
Oliver ________ once a week.

8 A company is redesigning our garden.
We ________.

c Complete the second sentence so that it means the same as the first sentence.

1 It is known that the thief is a local man.
The thief is known to be a local man.

2 The blackmailer is understood to be a colleague of the victim.
It is understood that the blackmailer is a colleague of the victim.

3 It is expected that the man will be acquitted.
The man ________.

4 It is reported that kidnappers have taken the president's wife.
Kidnappers ________.

5 The terrorists are thought to be hiding in the countryside.
It is ________.

6 The suspect is known to be dangerous.
It is ________.

7 The police are said to have arrested three men.
It is ________.

8 It is reported that vandals have damaged several buildings in the area.
Vandals ________.

d Write an anecdote about a crime that you or someone you know was affected by. Use the passive and causative *have*.

8B Faking it

G reporting verbs
V the media
P word stress

1 GRAMMAR reporting verbs

a Circle the correct form.

1 I agreed *to meet* / *meeting* my old school friend under the clock in the station.
2 My husband denied *to eat* / *eating* the last cream cake.
3 Maya promised *to give back* / *giving back* my book the next day.
4 The tour guide recommended *to visit* / *visiting* the Picasso Museum.
5 The girl refused *to dance* / *dancing* with my friend.
6 The police accused him *to commit* / *of committing* fraud.
7 My boyfriend asked me *to take* / *taking* him to the airport.
8 The teacher threatened *to give* / *giving* them extra homework if they didn't stop talking.
9 Nina's parents told her *not to be* / *not being* late.
10 The woman admitted *to steal* / *stealing* the man's watch.

b Complete the sentences reporting the direct speech using a reporting verb from the list.

~~advise~~ apologize insist invite offer remind suggest warn

1 'I really don't think you should leave your job,' Diego's friend told him.
Diego's friend advised him not to leave his job.
2 'I'm going with you to the doctor's, whether you like it or not,' Alice said to me.
Alice ______ to the doctor's with me, whether I liked it or not.
3 'Why don't we go for a walk?' said Katie.
Katie ______ for a walk.
4 'Shall I make the lunch?' her husband said.
Her husband ______ the lunch.
5 'Don't park there,' the man said to us. 'You'll get a fine.'
The man ______ there or we'd get a fine.
6 'I'm sorry I was so rude,' I said.
I ______ so rude.
7 'Would you like to have dinner with me?' Andy asked Sarah.
Andy ______ with him.
8 'Don't forget to sign the documents,' my boss told me.
My boss ______ the documents.

c Write about six things that people have said to you today. Use the reporting verbs from a and b.

1 ______
2 ______
3 ______
4 ______
5 ______
6 ______

2 PRONUNCIATION word stress

a **Underline the stressed syllable in the reporting verbs in the list. Then put them in the correct column.**

~~a|ccuse~~ ad|mit ad|vise a|gree con|vince de|ny in|sist in|vite o|ffer or|der per|suade pro|mise re|fuse re|gret re|mind su|ggest threa|ten

Stress on first syllable	Stress on second syllable
	accuse

b 8.2 **Listen and check. Then listen and repeat the reporting verbs.**

c 8.3 **Listen and complete the sentences.**

1 She *offered* *to* make the lunch.
2 He ______ ______ tidy his room.
3 They ______ ______ call the police.
4 She ______ ______ come home early.
5 They ______ ______ give me more time.
6 He ______ ______ her for his behaviour.

d **Listen again and repeat the sentences. Try to link the verbs and *to* where appropriate.**

3 VOCABULARY the media

a **Complete the headlines with a verb from the list that means the same as the verb in brackets.**

~~axed~~ back bids clash fall for hit quiz rows rush split vows wed

1 TV series *axed* after drop in audience figures (cut)
2 Singer to ______ Brazilian model (marry)
3 Celebrities ______ social media hoax (believe)
4 Police ______ wife after man disappears (question)
5 Hollywood stars ______ presidential candidate (support)
6 US stock market ______ by new company scandal (badly affected)
7 Firefighters ______ to stop fire in shopping centre (hurry)
8 Government ______ to invest more money in rural areas (promises)
9 Company director ______ with managers over treatment of staff (argues)
10 Celebrity couple ______ after five years (separate)
11 Former lawyer ______ to become country's new president (attempts)
12 Players ______ over referee's decision (disagree)

b **Complete the sentences with a media job from the list.**

agony aunt   commentator   critics   editor   freelance journalist   newsreader   ~~paparazzi~~   presenter   reporter

1 The *paparazzi* __________ were waiting outside the restaurant to photograph the princess.

2 Have you ever written an email to an __________, asking for advice?

3 I'm surprised none of the __________ liked the film; I thought it was great!

4 The __________ got very excited when the first goal was scored.

5 A __________ at the scene of the crime gave more details about the murder.

6 The newspaper __________ decided not to print the reporter's story because it was too politically sensitive.

7 I've stopped watching that chat show because I can't stand the __________.

8 Laura writes articles for different newspapers as a __________.

9 The __________ looked very serious when he announced that the politician had been shot.

c **Complete the sentences.**

1 The newspaper my father reads is bi*ased* __________ towards the government.

2 It's impossible for a journalist to be ob__________ about a subject on which he or she holds a strong opinion.

3 The article was cen__________ because it was too critical of the president.

4 Online papers use sen__________ headlines to make people click on an article and read it.

5 The reporter gave an acc__________ description of events; that's exactly how I remember them.

4 VOCABULARY FROM READING

Complete the chart with the words in the list according to their meaning.

~~doctored~~   exaggerated   improbable   legitimate   misleading   reliable   reputable   untrustworthy

Can be trusted	Can't be trusted
	doctored

9A The art of persuasion

G clauses of contrast and purpose
V advertising; business
P changing stress on nouns and verbs

1 GRAMMAR clauses of contrast and purpose

a Circle the correct word.

1 The restaurant staff seem happy *despite* / *although* the fact that they work long hours every day.
2 The account manager called his client *for* / *to* arrange a meeting.
3 The company is expanding *even though* / *in spite of* there is a recession.
4 The firm made several people redundant *in order to* / *so that* cut costs.
5 *Although* / *Despite* she's the head of the department, she often goes out with her colleagues after work.
6 I stayed at my desk *to not* / *so as not to* miss an important phone call.
7 Everybody seemed to enjoy Mike's speech at the wedding, *in spite of* / *even though* his terrible jokes.
8 She closed the door of her office *so as to* / *so that* nobody could hear her conversation.
9 I still buy that chocolate bar, *in spite of* / *though* it's much smaller than it used to be.
10 Yuri has to learn English *to* / *for* his job.

b Complete the second sentence so that it has a similar meaning to the first sentence. Use the **bold** word or phrase.

1 Is that a machine to make juice?
for
Is that a machine *for making juice* ?
2 The shop closed down even though it was in an ideal location.
in spite of
The shop closed down ______.
3 They reduced their prices so as to sell more products.
so that
They reduced their prices ______.
4 I have to leave by six o'clock so that I don't miss my train.
in order not to
I have to leave by six o'clock ______.
5 Despite the fact that I was very late, my boss wasn't angry.
although
My boss wasn't angry ______.
6 Although she's the manager, she doesn't have her own office.
despite
She doesn't have her own office ______.

2 **VOCABULARY** advertising; business

a Complete the sentences with a word from the list.

advertising agency   brand   campaign
consumer   jingle   podcast   pop-up   slogan
spam   ~~targeted advertising~~

1. *Targeted advertising* means that you'll receive hundreds of adverts for footwear if you buy some boots online.
2. As a ________, I want to have as much information as possible about the food I buy.
3. I always buy the same ________ of toothpaste because it's the one I'm used to.
4. They've used young adults in their new ________ because it's aimed specifically at people in their early 20s.
5. I heard their new ________ this morning, and now I can't forget it!
6. Nike's company ________ only has three words: *Just do it*.
7. Lucia's got a new job at an ________ in Liverpool. She's working on an advertisement for a pet food company.
8. Everybody's talking about it. In fact, I've heard that it's the most streamed sports ________ so far this year.
9. I've just installed a program that will stop any ________ from reaching my inbox.
10. It's annoying when a ________ blocks you from seeing what's on your computer screen.

b Read the definitions and complete the missing letters in the words.

1. the main office of a company
   h *e* *a* d o *f* *f* *i* c *e*
2. stop trading or doing business
   cl__ __ __ d__w__
3. an office or a shop / store belonging to a large company or organization
   br__n__ __
4. a difficult time for the economy of a country
   a r__c__ __ __i__ __
5. a period of sudden economic growth
   a b__o__
6. fall; become lower or less
   d__o__
7. make goods in large quantities, using machinery
   m__n__ __ __ __t__ __ __
8. combine to form a single thing
   m__ __g__

c Complete the text with the correct form of the verbs and verb phrases in the list.

become the market leader   expand   export   grow
import   market   produce   ~~set up a new business~~
take over

A friend of mine, Anne, was lucky enough to inherit a farm when she left university, so she decided to [1] *set up a new business*: an organic food company. The company [2] ________ its products under the name Anne's Fields, and among other things, it [3] ________ muesli. Anne [4] ________ nuts and dried fruit from South America and mixes these with cereal from crops on the farm to make the muesli. Her muesli sells well nationally, and recently she [5] ________ into new markets abroad. Today, she also [6] ________ to northern European countries, like Norway and Sweden.

The company is [7] ________ rapidly, and Anne is always looking for new employees. Right now, she's preparing to launch a new cereal bar the company has been testing. Anne is very realistic, as she knows she will never [8] ________ in the industry. However, neither does she want one of the big cereal giants to [9] ________ her small family company.

d Complete the sentences with the correct form of *make* or *do*.

1. A company always *does* extensive market research before it launches a new product.
2. If a company ________ a loss, the staff often face job cuts.
3. It's been a pleasure ________ business with you.
4. The managing director ________ the decision to close the factory yesterday.
5. The factory is going to ________ 30 people redundant after Christmas.
6. My company ________ really badly last year; if the situation doesn't improve, it may close.
7. Management and unions have ________ a deal that should prevent a strike.
8. If we ________ a profit again next year, the manager may think of opening another office.
9. There's no need to thank me. I'm only ________ my job.
10. She doesn't ________ much money from acting, so she's also got a part-time job as a waiter.

e Match 1–8 to responses a–h.

1 Where have you been? c
2 Shall we start the meeting? ___
3 I'm going out with my boss for a drink tonight. ___
4 Let's go to that lovely old café on the corner. ___
5 Shall we finish now? ___
6 Who are you messaging? ___
7 Your boss is heading in this direction. ___
8 Why do you need to talk to your ex? ___

a Yes, let's get down to business.
b I'm afraid it's gone out of business.
~~c Mind your own business!~~
d Are you sure you want to mix business with pleasure?
e OK, but first, is there any other business?
f I'm sorry, but it's none of your business.
g Because we have some unfinished business.
h Yes, and it looks as if she means business.

f Answer the questions about yourself and your home.

1 How far from your home is the nearest branch of your bank?

____

____

2 Which products are manufactured in your country?

____

____

3 Which companies from your country are market leaders?

____

____

4 Which products does your country export and where to?

____

____

5 Which industries are growing in your country?

____

____

6 Which products does your country import and where from?

____

____

7 Would you like to set up your own company? Why (not)?

____

____

3 PRONUNCIATION changing stress on nouns and verbs

a Underline the stressed syllable in the highlighted words.

1 China exports more goods than any other country.
2 They transport most of their products by lorry.
3 There's been a huge increase in petrol prices recently.
4 The price of wheat has decreased by 5%.
5 Scientists are making progress in finding a cure for AIDS.
6 The visa permits you to stay for three months.
7 Brazil produces about a third of the world's coffee.
8 We do not give refunds without a valid receipt.
9 The government is hoping to reduce foreign imports.
10 Vinyl records are becoming popular again.

b 9.1 Listen and check. Then listen again and repeat the sentences.

9B Dream cities

G uncountable and plural nouns
V word building: prefixes and suffixes
P word stress with prefixes and suffixes

1 GRAMMAR uncountable and plural nouns

a Circle the correct answers. Tick (✓) if both answers are possible.

1 Can I have *a piece of bread* / *some bread*, please? ✓
2 My grandmother suffers from *bad health* / *a bad health*.
3 I've bought *a new piece of furniture* / *some new furniture* for my living room.
4 Did we bring *a pair of scissors* / *a scissors*? I want to cut my nails.
5 I'm looking for *a cheap accommodation* / *some cheap accommodation*.
6 Jackie is upset because she's had *a bad news* / *some bad news*.
7 Be careful with that vase – it's made of *glass* / *a glass*.
8 My girlfriend gave me *a pair of pyjamas* / *some pyjamas* for my birthday.
9 The teacher gave the boy extra marks for *a good behaviour* / *good behaviour*.
10 Can you lend me *a paper* / *some paper*? I've left my notebook at home.

b Complete the sentences with *is* or *are*.

1 My clothes *are* really wet. I got caught in a thunderstorm.
2 Police ______ investigating the murder of an elderly woman in her home.
3 The hotel staff ______ always really polite and helpful.
4 The new research into sleep patterns ______ fascinating.
5 The outskirts of the town ______ quite run down and a bit depressing.
6 The good news ______ that we're getting married in the spring!
7 The flight crew on this plane ______ very young.
8 Politics ______ really fascinating – particularly for politicians!
9 Do you think my belongings ______ safe in the hotel room?
10 The traffic ______ terrible in the rush hour in the city centre.

c Complete the sentences with information that's true for you.

1 The scenery in this area ______________________.
2 The traffic in my area ______________________.
3 My clothes ______________________.
4 The furniture in my home ______________________.
5 The news today ______________________.
6 Politics in my country ______________________.
7 The weather today ______________________.
8 My family ______________________.

2 **VOCABULARY** word building: prefixes and suffixes

a Complete the sentences with a prefix from the list.

anti auto bi mega mis mono multi over post ~~sub~~ under

1 Some of the housing in the city is *sub*___standard. The apartments are of very poor quality.
2 There was a food shortage in many countries during the ______-war period between 1946 and 1960.
3 Hundreds of fans were waiting for the singer, hoping to get an ______graph.
4 My English teacher recommends us to use a ______lingual dictionary – one that is only in English.
5 My colleagues are always complaining that they are ______worked and ______paid. They say they work long hours and are badly paid.
6 The leader of the protest used a ______phone to make himself heard.
7 You couldn't miss Sandra – she was the one in the ______coloured coat. It was green, purple, yellow, and orange, I think.
8 The town has just celebrated its ______centenary – it was founded 200 years ago.
9 The doctor prescribed ______biotics for my brother's chest infection.
10 It's a popular ______conception that cold weather can give you a cold. This is simply not true.

b Complete the sentences. Add *-able*, *-ful*, *-less*, or *-proof* to a word from the list.

~~break~~ bullet care drink home hope use water

1 Is there anything *breakable*________ in this box?
2 Be ________________ crossing that road – there's always a lot of traffic.
3 Don't forget to take a ________________ jacket with you when you go walking in Scotland.
4 This ________________ gadget opens jars for people who lack strength in their hands.
5 Harry became ________________ when he was made redundant and could no longer pay his rent.
6 The police officer wasn't injured because he was wearing a ________________ vest.
7 Is the tap water ________________ in this area?
8 It's ________________ asking the boss for a pay rise – the company is losing money.

c Complete the sentences with the noun form of the word in brackets.

1 I borrowed the money with the *intention*________ of giving it back to you. (intend)
2 His greatest ________________ is his inability to express his feelings. (weak)
3 I was away for six months, and there were many changes in my ________________. (absent)
4 If you witness an act of ________________, you are advised to call the police. (vandal)
5 ________________ is one of the greatest problems in society today. (lonely)
6 Teachers are trying to fight ________________ in schools throughout the country. (race)
7 Most of her problems are the result of a very unhappy ________________. (child)
8 The best thing about our hotel was that it provided ________________ in the evenings. (entertain)
9 There's been a great ________________ in public transport recently. (improve)
10 There's a shortage of rented ________________ where I live. (accommodate)
11 What's the ________________ between Rome and Venice? (distant)
12 Gandhi was a humanist who believed we should all live in peace and ________________. (brother)

d **Complete the second sentence with the noun form of the bold word in the first sentence.**

1 I **believe** that house prices are going to rise.
It's my belief ____________ that house prices are going to rise.

2 The staff were shocked when their boss **died**.
The staff were shocked at the ____________ of their boss.

3 You shouldn't go out when it's **hot** in the day.
You shouldn't go out during the ____________ of the day.

4 You need to measure how **wide** the windows are.
You need to measure the ____________ of your windows.

5 I can't believe you're still **hungry** after that huge meal.
I can't believe that huge meal didn't satisfy your ____________.

6 The company may **lose** financially on this deal.
The company might make a financial ____________ on this deal.

7 Do you know how **high** Mount Kilimanjaro is?
Do you know the ____________ of Mount Kilimanjaro?

8 I don't like to **think** of you walking home alone.
I don't like the ____________ of you walking home alone.

9 After his illness, they gave him soup to make him **strong** again.
After his illness, they gave him soup to build up his ____________ again.

10 The dinner party was very **successful**.
The dinner party was a great ____________.

3 VOCABULARY FROM READING

Complete the sentences with a word or phrase from the list.

are unmatched   digital skills   going on every day of the week   committed to becoming a clean city   monitor traffic   ~~urban environments~~

1 We need to plant trees and have more green spaces in our urban environments ____________.

2 The council are planning to ____________ to see which roads are the busiest in this city.

3 I like spending time in Dublin because there's always lots ____________.

4 My sister is an IT teacher and really wants to help her students improve their ____________.

5 By reducing our carbon emissions, we're ____________ by the end of the decade.

6 The eco-friendly features of this product ____________ by anything that's made by other companies.

4 PRONUNCIATION word stress with prefixes and suffixes

a **Underline the main stressed syllable in the words in the list. Then put them in the correct column.**

~~an|ti|so|cial~~   bi|lin|gual   con|ve|ni|ence   en|ter|tain|ment   ex|cite|ment   friend|li|ness   go|vern|ment   ig|no|rance   o|ver|crow|ded   po|ver|ty   re|duc|tion   un|em|ploy|ment

Stress on first syllable	Stress on second syllable	Stress on third syllable
		antisocial

b 9.2 **Listen and check. Then listen and repeat the words.**

English File talks to...
George Tannenbaum
Advertising executive

1 LOOKING AT LANGUAGE

Complete the sentences with a metaphor or idiomatic expression from the list.

a captive audience get into your head had their day ~~hit a false note~~ word for word

1 The mayor hit a false note ______ with her speech and caused a lot of controversy.
2 Some people say that libraries have ______ and they will soon disappear.
3 The song has a catchy chorus which can easily ______ and you find yourself singing it all day.
4 Musicians often play on trains and ask for money because they know they have ______.
5 I repeated her instructions ______ to avoid any confusion.

2 VOCABULARY FROM THE INTERVIEW

Complete the sentences from the interview with a word or phrase from the list.

baton ~~cerebral~~ courant earworms passé their ears perk up pixelize

1 I tend not to be funny in TV commercials...partly because I am a kind of cerebral ______ guy.
2 ...and people, you know, ______ when they see a celebrity.
3 ...you remember them... – what do they call them, ______?
4 I don't think something as kind of ______ as a billboard will be dead as long as, like, the highways are crowded.
5 And until we can kind of ______ ourselves and beam ourselves to work, I think there will be billboards.
6 My father kind of took the ______ from him.
7 I know it's, like, '______' to say, 'I don't have a TV' or 'I never watch TV', but people do.

3 THE CONVERSATION

Match beginnings 1–3 to endings a–c.

1 ...and you're being influenced, so, for example we, b
2 You know, we barely, ______
3 ...they're starting to be ______

a we don't really watch TV...
b ~~we all know certain brands just because they're everywhere around us.~~
c – my 11-year-old is starting to become a little bit more cynical about what he sees....

4 VOCABULARY FROM THE CONVERSATION

Match the words from the conversation to the definitions a–e.

1 blatant e
2 point ______
3 rush ______
4 subliminally ______
5 subtle ______

a when you are in a hurry and need to do things quickly
b in a way that affects your mind, even though you are not aware of it
c done in a clever way, and using indirect methods, in order to achieve something
d the purpose or aim of something
e ~~done in an obvious and open way without caring if people are shocked~~

1-9 Can you remember...?

GRAMMAR & VOCABULARY

a Complete the second sentence so that it means the same as the first sentence. Write two to five words. Use the word in brackets.

1 Owen started studying at 9.00 a.m. and he's still studying now, at 6.00 p.m. (has)
Owen ______________________________ all day.

2 We aren't very keen on climbing, so we didn't go to the mountains. (much)
We didn't go to the mountains because we don't like ______________________________.

3 I don't have Harry's number, so I can't call him. (his)
I'd call Harry if I ______________________________.

4 Freya still finds it strange to live on her own. She really doesn't like it. (get)
Freya can't ______________________________ on her own. She really doesn't like it.

5 I can't wait to see you next week. (looking)
I'm ______________________________ next week.

6 I'll always remember the first time I visited Florence. I fell in love with the city. (forget)
I'll ______________________________ for the first time. I fell in love with the city.

7 I'm sure you left your jacket in the car. You weren't wearing it when you came in. (have)
You ______________________________ in the car. You weren't wearing it when you came in.

8 I get the impression that Emily has been crying. (as)
It ______________________________ has been crying.

9 We asked a local plumber to fit our shower. (had)
We ______________________________ by a local plumber.

10 His teacher said he should enter the writing competition. (encouraged)
His teacher ______________________________ the writing competition.

11 I arrived on time, although I had left home late. (despite)
______________________________, I arrived on time

12 Ash bought some new shorts in the sale. (a)
Ash bought ______________________________ in the sale.

b Complete the text. Write one word in each gap.

WORLD NEWS

Home | News | Sport | Weather

India set to break world records

It would seem that Tokyo is about to lose its position 1 __________ the largest city in the world. According to the UN, Delhi, the capital of India, is set to take the top spot in 2028. The organization predicts that Delhi's population will 2 __________ grown from 32.3 million to 39 million 3 __________ 2030. Meanwhile, it 4 __________ thought that Tokyo's population will remain at its current level of 37.3 million.

In 5 __________, this will not be the first time that India has broken a population record. In 2022, the country overtook China to become the most populous country in the world. India is currently home to around 1.45 billion people while China has around 1.42 billion. China's population appears to have reached its peak, while the population of India is expected 6 __________ continue growing until 2062.

Delhi is not the only city in India where significant population growth is predicted to 7 __________ place. The population of Mumbai is set to rise from 22 million to 25 million. In 8 __________ of this growth, the city will maintain its position as the world's sixth-largest city. 9 __________ though the population of Kolkata will increase from 16 million to 18 million, the city will move down the list, from 13th to 16th position. Bengaluru, which is ranked 27th 10 __________ the moment, will move up to the 21st spot as its population grows from 14 million to 16 million.

10A Eureka!

G quantifiers: *all*, *every*, *both*, etc.
V science
P stress in word families

1 VOCABULARY & PRONUNCIATION
science; stress in word families

a Circle a, b, or c.

1 He's working as a biology teacher although he's a qualified ______.
a zoology **b** zoologist **c** zoological

2 There are thousands of human ______ diseases.
a genetics **b** geneticist **c** genetic

3 My partner has a degree in ______.
a physics **b** physicist **c** physical

4 The results of ______ research have increased the range of medicines available to treat many illnesses.
a botany **b** botanist **c** botanical

5 I'm the only ______ in my family.
a science **b** scientist **c** scientific

6 I wasn't very good at ______ when I was at school.
a chemistry **b** chemist **c** chemical

7 It is thought that there is a ______ reason for his aggressive behaviour.
a biology **b** biologist **c** biological

8 My sister is fascinated by space and she's hoping to become an ______.
a astronomy **b** astronomer **c** astronomical

b Underline the stressed syllable in the words. Is the stress on the same syllable? Tick (✓) the correct column.

		same syllable	different syllable
1	a|stro|no|my / a|stro|no|mer	✓	
2	bi|o|lo|gy / bi|o|lo|gi|cal		
3	bo|ta|ny / bo|ta|ni|cal		
4	che|mist / che|mi|stry		
5	ge|ne|tic / ge|ne|ti|cist		
6	phy|sics / phy|si|cist		
7	sci|en|tist / sci|en|ti|fic		
8	zo|o|lo|gist / zo|o|lo|gic|al		

c 10.1 Listen and check. Then listen again and repeat the words.

d Complete the text with the nouns and verbs in the lists.

Verbs

carry out clone ~~do~~ prove volunteer

Nouns

clinical trials discovery drugs guinea pigs ~~pharmaceutical companies~~

Thousands of scientists are employed in 1 *pharmaceutical companies* to 2 *do* research into new 3 ______. These people hope to make an important 4 ______ which will help treat or cure an illness or disease. When a team believes they have developed a new drug, they have to 5 ______ experiments to 6 ______ their theory and make sure the drug is effective. The final stage of this process is to organize 7 ______ so that the drug can be tested on humans. People who 8 ______ to take part in these tests are known as 9 ______, after the animals that were used in 19th-century medical research. If the tests are successful, the drug is launched onto the market.

One branch of science that is becoming increasingly important in these companies is genetics. Genetic engineers have already managed to 10 ______ a number of different animals.

2 VOCABULARY FROM LISTENING

Match the words in the list to the definitions.

dissolve ~~gas~~ gravity moist particle
reflect rotate scatter water vapour

1 any substance like air that is neither a solid nor a liquid *gas* ___
2 mix with a liquid and become part of it ___
3 a very small piece of something ___
4 make things move very quickly in different directions ___
5 water in the form of a gas resulting from heating water or ice ___
6 show the image of somebody / something on the surface of, e.g., a mirror ___
7 slightly wet ___
8 move or turn around a central fixed point ___
9 the force that causes objects to fall to the ground when they are dropped ___

3 VOCABULARY FROM READING

Complete the sentences with the words from the list.

avatar bacteria genes implants laser
lithium ~~solar~~ sensors toxins

1 Some people have *solar* ___ panels installed on their roofs to save money on their energy bills.
2 Eye colour and blood type are passed on from parents to their children through their ___.
3 Most people use an ___ rather than a profile photo when they write posts in a chat room.
4 Some plants produce dangerous ___ that can seriously harm humans and animals.
5 Dentists use different kinds of ___ to replace missing teeth in the mouth.
6 Electric car manufacturers need large quantities of ___ to make batteries for their vehicles.
7 It's important to cook meat to a high enough temperature to kill any harmful ___.
8 The surgeons used a ___ to perform the operation on my eye.
9 The security lights come on when the ___ detect a movement nearby.

4 GRAMMAR quantifiers: *all*, *every*, *both*, etc.

a Right (✓) or wrong (✗)? Correct the mistakes in the highlighted phrases.

1 I've taken all luggage up to our room, OK? *✗ all the luggage*
2 Everybody were bad-tempered because it was getting late and they were hungry. ___
3 All went wrong at my last job interview. ___
4 I have a lot of cousins, but most of them live abroad. ___
5 Every classroom in that school has an interactive whiteboard. ___
6 My mum works as a volunteer at the hospital every morning. ___
7 The most people are against eating genetically modified food. ___
8 All the dogs should be on a lead in public spaces. ___

b **Complete the conversations with *no*, *any*, or *none*.**

1 **A** Can I have a biscuit?
B Sorry, we don't have *any* __________.

2 **A** How much homework have you done?
B __________. I don't feel like doing it right now.

3 **A** How are we going to get home?
B By taxi. There aren't __________ buses at this time of night.

4 **A** Did any of your friends pass the exam?
B No, __________ of them. It was too difficult.

5 **A** Shall we have dinner in our hotel room?
B We can't. There's __________ room service after 9 p.m.

6 **A** When can you come?
B __________ day you like. I'm free all week.

c **Complete the sentences with a word from the list. Use each word twice.**

both either neither nor

1 *Both* __________ my brother and my sister have children.
2 Dave has two sons, but __________ of them looks like him.
3 We'd like to go to __________ Greece or Portugal for our holiday this year.
4 Neither my boyfriend __________ I eat meat.
5 I can't decide between these two shirts. I like __________ of them.
6 __________ of my parents have ever been to South America.
7 My niece is studying __________ chemistry or biology at university – I can't remember which.
8 Her husband neither calls __________ messages her when he's away.

d **Complete the text. Write one word in each gap.**

Irène and Ève Curie: the scientist and the journalist

Nearly [1] *everyone* __________ knows the names of scientists Marie and Pierre Curie because of the Nobel Prizes they won. However, [2] __________ people are unaware that the couple also had two talented daughters, Irène and Ève. [3] __________ sisters received the same education, but they each pursued a completely different career.

Irène followed in the footsteps of her parents. She began assisting her mother during the First World War, when she was only 18. The two women used some of the first X-ray machines to help doctors locate the exact position of soldiers' injuries. At the time, people had [4] __________ idea of the dangers posed by the machines, and nurses who used them didn't wear [5] __________ protection. As a result, Irène and her mother were exposed to large doses of radiation and [6] __________ of them lived to a very old age.

In 1924, Irène was asked to share her research techniques with a chemical engineer named Frédéric Joliot. They started going out together, but Marie was afraid that Joliot was only interested in becoming associated with the Curie name. She used [7] __________ her influence to try to end the relationship, but Irène took [8] __________ of her advice, and the couple later married. Irène and her husband continued working together, and in 1935 they too were awarded a Nobel Prize.

Ève Curie, on the other hand, preferred the arts and spent most of her time [9] __________ writing or playing the piano. She worked as a journalist and wrote her mother's biography Madame Curie, which was published in 1937. Her husband, Henry Richardson Labouisse, was Executive Director of UNICEF, and when the organization was awarded the Nobel Peace Prize in 1965, he collected the award. Ève used to joke that [10] __________ member of her family had received a Nobel Prize except for her.

Irène Joliot-Curie died in Paris in 1956 at the age of 58. Ève Curie was 102 when she passed away in New York in 2007.

10B Freedom of speech

G articles
V collocation: word pairs
P pausing and sentence stress

1 GRAMMAR articles

a Complete the sayings with *a*, *an*, *the*, or no article (–).

1 All you need is __–__ love.
2 He's ______ man of his word
3 ______ time waits for no man.
4 Don't worry! It isn't ______ end of ______ world!
5 That's ______ life!
6 It's ______ small world!
7 ______ actions speak louder than ______ words.

b Complete the sentences with *the* where necessary.

1 __–__ Mount Aconcagua is in __the__ Andes in Argentina.
2 There are 50 states in ______ USA.
3 ______ M1 motorway was closed yesterday because of floods.
4 ______ Royal Lancaster Hotel is near ______ Hyde Park in London.
5 ______ Dodecanese are a group of islands situated in ______ Aegean Sea.
6 ______ Lake Victoria is the largest lake in ______ Africa.
7 ______ Panama Canal connects the Atlantic Ocean to ______ Pacific Ocean.
8 The toy industry in ______ China is the biggest in the world.

c Right (✓) or wrong (✗)? Correct the mistakes in the highlighted phrases.

1 The church in my village dates back to the 15th century. __✓__
2 My grandfather is in the hospital having an operation. __✗ in hospital__
3 The university in my town has a very good reputation. ______
4 Daisy is taking advantage of the time her children are at the school to do an online course. ______
5 The prison is on the outskirts of the city. ______
6 Somebody broke into my parents' house while they were at the church. ______
7 We caught the bus from the stop near the hospital. ______
8 My boyfriend is at the university. He's studying architecture. ______
9 The man has gone to the prison for the crimes he committed when he was younger. ______
10 My brother teaches at the school he went to when he was a child. ______

d Read the article. Circle a, b, or c.

Five words that made history

At the 2018 Golden Globe Awards, actress and TV presenter Oprah Winfrey was awarded the Cecil B. DeMille Award for lifetime achievement. Here is an extract from the memorable speech she made during the award ceremony.

In 1964, I was [1]____ little girl sitting on the linoleum floor of my mother's house in [2]____ Milwaukee, watching Anne Bancroft present the Oscar for Best Actor at [3]____ 36th Academy Awards. She opened the envelope and said five words that literally made [4]____ history: '[5]____ winner is Sidney Poitier.' Up to the stage came [6]____ most elegant man I had ever seen. I remember his tie was white and, of course, his skin was black. And I'd never seen [7]____ black man being celebrated like that. And I have tried many, many, many times to explain what [8]____ moment like that means to a little girl, a kid watching from the cheap seats as my mom came through the door, bone tired from cleaning [9]____ other people's houses. But all I can do is quote and say that [10]____ explanation's in Sidney's performance in *Lilies of the Field*, 'Amen, amen. Amen, amen.'

1	**a** a	**b** the	**c** –
2	**a** a	**b** the	**c** –
3	**a** a	**b** the	**c** –
4	**a** a	**b** the	**c** –
5	**a** A	**b** The	**c** –
6	**a** a	**b** the	**c** –
7	**a** a	**b** the	**c** –
8	**a** a	**b** the	**c** –
9	**a** a	**b** the	**c** –
10	**a** a	**b** the	**c** –

2 VOCABULARY collocation: word pairs

a Match questions 1–10 to responses a–j.

1. Did you hear the storm last night? h
2. Do you think I should accept the job? ____
3. Why are you moving to the country? ____
4. Why has the shop sold out of bread? ____
5. How was your meeting? ____
6. What did you do while you were waiting at the hospital? ____
7. Why does water boil when you heat it? ____
8. What should I do about the argument I had with my sister? ____
9. Why is the playground closed? ____
10. My bike was stolen because I forgot to lock it up. ____

a I'd forgive and forget if I were you.
b Oh well, you live and learn, I suppose.
c I paced backwards and forwards in the corridor.
d You need to weigh up the pros and cons to help you make a decision.
e It's the law of cause and effect.
f I guess it's a question of supply and demand.
g Short and sweet – it only lasted ten minutes.
~~h Yes, the thunder and lightning woke me up.~~
i We're looking for some peace and quiet.
j For health and safety reasons.

b Find the word pairs in the list and link them with *or*. Then complete the sentences.

~~alive~~ all ~~dead~~ later less more never nothing now once rain right shine sooner twice wrong

1 The criminal was wanted *dead or alive* ________ and there was a $500 reward for his capture.
2 She goes jogging every morning, ________________.
3 I'm not sure if this answer in my maths homework is ________________.
4 Patricia is about to leave, so it's ________________ – I may not get another chance to ask her out.
5 It's ________________ with Sue; either she calls every day or you don't hear from her for weeks.
6 I've been skiing ________________, but I'm not very good at it.
7 Nathan has ________________ finished his homework – all he has to do now is to print it out.
8 There's no point waiting – I'll have to tell John the truth ________________.

c Complete the word-pair idioms.

1 We only take a few b*its* ________ and p*ieces* ________ with us when we go on holiday.
2 I'm s________ and t________ of having to tidy up after my children.
3 B________ and l________, I'd say I had a happy childhood.
4 She's fine now, but it was t________ and g________ whether she would survive the operation.
5 The streets were very dangerous because of the lack of l________ and o________ in the city.
6 We arrived s________ and s________ after a difficult three-day journey through the mountains.
7 I've no idea what we're having for my birthday lunch because my wife told me to w________ and s________.
8 We go to the cinema n________ and a________, but more often than not, we just watch a film on TV.

3 VOCABULARY FROM READING

Complete the missing vowels in the words and phrases.

1 A speaker doesn't have to be a comedian to include a little w_*i*_t in his or her speech.
2 Salespeople need to have the g___ft of the g___b to sell as many products as possible.
3 That politician is very good at making memorable s_____nd b___t___s when he talks to journalists.
4 Winston Churchill was famous for being a great ___r___t___r who made powerful speeches.

4 PRONUNCIATION pausing and sentence stress

a 10.2 Listen to a talk about an interesting place to visit. Mark the pauses.

Good morning, and thank you for coming. I'm here to talk about an interesting place to visit in my country. I'm going to tell you about the city of Bath in the south-west of England. Bath is on the River Avon, and it has one of the only bridges in the world with shops on either side. The city is famous for its ancient Roman Baths, which can still be visited today. It has many beautiful streets, such as the Royal Crescent and the Circus. Bath is full of museums, independent shops, and wonderful places to eat and drink. The city is easily accessible from London by train, and it is perfect for a day trip or a weekend break.

b Practise giving the talk, pausing and trying to get the right rhythm.

c Now write your own talk about an interesting place to visit in your country. Mark the pauses.

d Read your speech. If you can, record it on your phone and send it to your teacher.

Answer Key

1A

1 GRAMMAR

a 3 ✗ Where do you usually go
4 ✓
5 ✗ What happened
6 ✓
7 ✓
8 ✗ Whose jacket did you borrow
9 ✗ Should we go now
10 ✗ Who are you waiting for?

b 2 where the lift is
3 where we parked the car
4 if there are any tickets left for the concert tonight
5 what time the match starts
6 when Fatima's birthday is
7 what Jamie does for a living
8 where Natalie lives
9 what Ava's boyfriend's name is
10 how much you paid for your new car

c 2 Who cooks in your family?
3 When did your brother pass his driving test?
4 Do you know who's going to the party tonight?
5 Who's the manager talking to now?
6 Who ate the chocolates I left in the cupboard?
7 Why didn't you come to school yesterday?
8 Do you remember what time the meeting is?

d Students' own answers

2 PRONUNCIATION

a 2 ✓, 4 ✓, 6 ✓

c **Expressions showing interest:** How interesting! Me too! Wow!
Expressions showing sympathy: I'm so sorry. Oh, really? What a shame!
Follow-up questions: Why? Why do you say that? Why is that?

e 2 Why do you say that?
3 I'm so sorry.
4 Why is that?
5 Wow!
6 What a shame!

3 VOCABULARY

a 2 play ball
3 stick at
4 have something up your sleeve
5 move on
6 print off

b 2 look the part, 3 come in handy, 4 stand out, 5 do your homework, 6 come up, 7 steer clear, 8 put together

1B

1 GRAMMAR

a (unnecessary words at the end of the sentences)
2 love that book
3 listening to the instructions
4 believe in ghosts
5 going to the party
6 always lock the front door
7 visited a nutritionist
8 already heard the story

b 2 do, would
3 haven't, do
4 aren't, have
5 Will, won't
6 could, have
7 did, was
8 are, do

c Students' own answers

2 PRONUNCIATION

a 2 weren't, Weren't, were
3 didn't, Didn't, did
4 was, Were, wasn't
5 won't, will, won't
6 can, Can, can't

3 GRAMMAR IN CONTEXT

2 more interesting, more likely
3 later, more difficult
4 further, colder
5 more qualified, higher
6 bigger, longer

4 VOCABULARY

a 2 open-minded, 3 tight-fisted, 4 absent-minded, 5 strong-willed, 6 laid-back, 7 well-balanced, 8 big-headed, 9 narrow-minded, 10 two-faced, 11 good-tempered, 12 self-centred, 13 easy-going, 14 well-behaved

b 2 laid-back, 3 well-balanced, 4 narrow-minded, 5 self-centred, 6 two-faced, 7 open-minded, 8 strong-willed, 9 tight-fisted, 10 big-headed, 11 absent-minded, 12 well-behaved, 13 good-tempered, 14 bad-tempered

c Students' own answers

5 VOCABULARY FROM READING

2 extraordinary, 3 remote, 4 trace, 5 puzzle, 6 baffle

Colloquial English 1

1 LOOKING AT LANGUAGE

2 c, 3 a, 4 b, 5 d

2 VOCABULARY FROM THE INTERVIEW

2 talk sb's language, 3 jargon, 4 give sb an easy ride, 5 graduate trainee, 6 delivery, 7 stay on your brief

3 THE CONVERSATION

2 definitely, 3 really, 4 will

4 VOCABULARY FROM THE CONVERSATION

2 potentially, 3 white, 4 caught, 5 willing

Can you remember...? 1

GRAMMAR & VOCABULARY

a 3 does this phone belong
4 didn't you like
5 Who gave you
6 how much petrol costs
7 tell me whether you have
8 won't you
9 neither can my friends
10 does know about the meeting

b 1 b, 2 b, 3 b, 4 c, 5 c, 6 b, 7 c, 8 c, 9 b, 10 a

2A

1 VOCABULARY

a 2 sunburn, 3 being sick, 4 bleeding, 5 swollen, 6 sneezing, 7 cough, 8 headache, 9 hurts, 10 temperature

b 2 flu, 3 cut yourself, 4 fainted, 5 blister, 6 sore throat, 7 feels sick, 8 cold, 9 dizzy

c 2 unconscious, 3 sprained, 4 blood pressure, 5 food poisoning, 6 choking, 7 burnt

d 2 f, 3 d, 4 a, 5 b, 6 c

e 2 over, 3 out, 4 up, 5 round

f 1 tip, 2 ice pack, 3 heat pack, 4 rub, 5 push up, 6 bandage

g Students' own answers

2 VOCABULARY FROM READING

2 heart rate
3 worst-case scenario
4 life-threatening illness
5 under the weather
6 open-heart surgery
7 scare stories

3 PRONUNCIATION

a 2 specialist, 3 finger, 4 stomach, 5 couch, 6 negative

4 GRAMMAR

a 3 ✓
4 ✓
5 we've run out of painkillers
6 ✓
7 How long have you known
8 Sasha's been coughing all day
9 ✓
10 have you fainted recently

b 2 have you eaten
3 he hasn't been sleeping
4 I have / I've just burnt
5 I have / 've been having
6 I have / I've ever met
7 Georgia hasn't been going
8 Jamie has had
9 has your girlfriend been looking for
10 I haven't read

c 2 haven't been feeling
3 have / 've had
4 haven't been
5 have / 've been lying
6 has / 's been looking after
7 have / 've been thinking
8 have / 've come up with
9 have / 've been trying
10 haven't managed

d Students' own answers

Answer Key

2B

1 VOCABULARY

a 2 hooded, 3 long-sleeved, 4 checked, 5 tight, 6 patterned, 7 spotted, 8 loose, 9 polo-neck, 10 V-neck, 11 sleeveless, 12 striped

b 2 cotton, 3 lace, 4 leather, 5 linen, 6 silk, 7 suede, 8 velvet, 9 fur, 10 Lycra, 11 woollen

c 2 classic, 3 casual, 4 scruffy, 5 old-fashioned

d 2 d, 3 g, 4 b, 5 h, 6 a, 7 c, 8 e

e Students' own answers

2 PRONUNCIATION

a 2 striped, 3 shorts, 4 fit, 5 leather

3 GRAMMAR

a 2 tight red, 3 cheap Lycra, 4 long checked, 5 brand new purple, 6 stylish grey, 7 blue suede, 8 smart red

b
2 I'm looking for a classic black dress.
3 He often wears a long-sleeved checked shirt.
4 They gave me a beautiful French lace top.
5 Have you got a plain yellow T-shirt I can borrow?
6 This pink hooded jacket is on offer.
7 I'm not a fan of tight polo-neck sweaters.
8 Vincent is the one in the strange fur hat.

c
3 ✗ white leather trousers
4 ✗ scruffy old jeans
5 ✓
6 ✗ new grey Armani suit
7 ✓
8 ✗ trendy purple glasses

d
2 I met an interesting French woman at the party.
3 My sister has lovely long black hair.
4 Ava's just bought an expensive striped silk top.
5 There's a beautiful round wooden table in my friend's kitchen.
6 Max gave his girlfriend an unusual gold ring for her birthday.
7 My boss drives a powerful red Italian sports car.
8 We've been having some awful wet weather recently.

3A

1 VOCABULARY

a 2 rear, 3 approximately, 4 requiring, 5 proceed to, 6 disembark, 7 place, 8 locate

b 2 bag drop, 3 customs, 4 gate, 5 check-in desk, 6 runway, 7 airport terminal, 8 flight times, 9 security, 10 baggage reclaim

c 2 trolley, 3 arrivals, 4 first class, 5 luggage, 6 illegal goods, 7 collect, 8 delayed

d 2 connecting flight, 3 boarding pass, 4 Departures, 5 hand luggage, 6 scanning, 7 checked, 8 liquids, 9 sharp objects, 10 departures board, 11 boarding, 12 delayed, 13 take off, 14 on time, 15 board, 16 land

e 2 row, 3 direct flight, 4 seat belt, 5 long-haul flight, 6 cabin crew, 7 turbulence, 8 jet lag

f 2 a, 3 c, 4 b, 5 c, 6 a

g 2 in, 3 off, 4 in, 5 on, 6 up, 7 off, 8 off

h Students' own answers

2 VOCABULARY FROM READING

2 low-cost
3 tail
4 evacuation
5 altitude
6 special assistance
7 engine
8 overhead locker

3 GRAMMAR IN CONTEXT

2 such a, 3 so many, 4 such, 5 so much, 6 such, 7 so

4 GRAMMAR

a
3 had been looking
4 had picked up
5 had been sitting
6 ✓
7 had cancelled
8 ✓

b
2 arrived
3 was raining
4 left
5 went
6 got
7 looked
8 had / 'd already checked in
9 were waiting
10 had / 'd given
11 called
12 had / 'd already gone
13 had / 'd been waiting
14 had been reading
15 had been doing

c Students' own answers

5 PRONUNCIATION

b 2 sang, 3 paid, 4 met, 5 wore, 6 woke, 7 told, 8 flew, 9 stood, 10 said

c 2 flying, 3 five, 4 music, 5 husband, 6 suddenly, 7 noise, 8 sounded, 9 pilot, 10 happened

3B

1 GRAMMAR

a 2 in fact, 3 absolutely, 4 hard, 5 sometimes, 6 straight away

b
2 My daughter is hardly ever ill.
3 His parents are retiring next year.
4 The boy was extremely rude to his teacher.
5 My sister dresses very stylishly.
6 Apparently, James is getting divorced.
7 I would never have thought you were 30.
8 His ankle was bandaged carefully by a nurse.
9 I'll be there in five minutes.
10 I go to bed much later in the summer.

c
2 Although she studies a lot, she rarely goes to the library.
3 Unfortunately, I crashed my new car last week.
4 Ideally, we should leave early tomorrow.
5 I can hardly understand a word when people speak English quickly.
6 Kevin nearly forgot his doctor's appointment yesterday.
7 She's incredibly angry because her husband came home late last night.
8 Surprisingly, it didn't rain at all while we were in London.

2 VOCABULARY

a 2 lately, 3 especially, 4 nearly, 5 yet, 6 hardly, 7 ever, 8 near, 9 hard, 10 specially, 11 at the moment, 12 at the end, 13 late, 14 in the end, 15 actually, 16 still

b 2 Ideally, 3 certainly, 4 gradually, 5 eventually, 6 in fact, 7 Obviously, 8 Apparently

c 2 fast, 3 One day, 4 harder, 5 probably, 6 Eagerly, 7 alone, 8 At long last, 9 Unfortunately, 10 extremely, 11 angrily, 12 together, 13 enviously

d Students' own answers

3 PRONUNCIATION

a **Stress on first syllable:** actually, basically, definitely, fortunately, gradually, luckily, obviously

Stress on second syllable: apparently, especially, eventually, ideally, incredibly, unfortunately

Stress on third syllable: absolutely

c
2 actually, married
3 unfortunately, extremely
4 incredibly, sad
5 definitely, ideally
6 Apparently, parents

Colloquial English 2

1 LOOKING AT LANGUAGE

2 doorstep, 3 key, 4 basis, 5 horizons, 6 words

2 VOCABULARY FROM THE INTERVIEW

2 convey a meaning, 3 pastime, 4 wannabe, 5 fairy tales, 6 illustrations, 7 creepy

3 THE CONVERSATION

2 and things like that, 3 sort of, 4 like

Answer Key

4 VOCABULARY FROM THE CONVERSATION

2 a clue, 3 out of it, 4 huge, 5 key to

Can you remember...? 1–3

GRAMMAR & VOCABULARY

a 1 narrow-minded, 2 swollen, 3 infection, 4 incredibly, 5 sleeveless / short-sleeved, 6 fashionable, 7 security, 8 arrivals, 9 specially, 10 gradually

b 1 b, 2 c, 3 c, 4 b, 5 a, 6 a, 7 b, 8 c, 9 c, 10 b

4A

1 GRAMMAR

a 2 will be travelling
3 won't have finished
4 will be having
5 will have had
6 will be leaving
7 will have gone
8 will be waiting

b 2 will be flying
3 will / 'll have done
4 will / 'll have read
5 will / 'll be playing
6 will / 'll have built
7 will / 'll have finished
8 will / 'll be driving
9 will have stopped
10 Will you be going

c 2 What will you be doing this time tomorrow?
3 What time will you be getting up tomorrow morning?
4 How much TV will you have watched by the end of this week?
5 Where will you be going next weekend?
6 When will you have finished your English homework?
7 How many times will you have looked at your phone by the end of today?
8 How many hours will you have spent studying English by the end of the week?

d Students' own answers

2 VOCABULARY

a 2 drought, 3 freezing, 4 chilly, 5 changeable, 6 warm

b 2 blizzard, 3 flood, 4 hail, 5 thunder, 6 drought, 7 monsoon, 8 lightning, 9 hurricane

c 2 g, 3 i, 4 e, 5 h, 6 a, 7 d, 8 f, 9 b

d 2 icy, 3 strong, 4 heavy, 5 hail, 6 mild, 7 showers, 8 sunny, 9 changeable, 10 breeze, 11 settled, 12 bright, 13 drizzling, 14 warm, 15 cool, 16 chilly, 17 mist, 18 clear, 19 damp, 20 pours

e Students' own answers

3 PRONUNCIATION

a 2 flood, 3 mist, 4 blow, 5 mild, 6 humid, 7 wear, 8 heat, 9 world, 10 pouring

4B

1 GRAMMAR

a 2 eat, 0
3 'll stay, 1
4 doesn't answer, 0
5 are, 0
6 won't move, 1
7 cooks, 1
8 doesn't come, 1

b 2 doesn't leave
3 don't take
4 is / 's studying
5 are / 're
6 will / 'll ask
7 haven't read
8 don't get

c 2 as soon as he arrives
3 unless the traffic
4 in case he forgets
5 before she goes
6 until you get
7 if I am / I'm
8 when I go

d Students' own answers

2 PRONUNCIATION

a 2 worth it in
3 and above all
4 In an ideal
5 unless it's
6 as soon as
7 As far as
8 such an awful

3 VOCABULARY

a 2 a, 3 f, 4 d, 5 c, 6 i, 7 j, 8 b, 9 h, 10 g

b 2 take advantage of
3 take part in
4 take your time
5 take place
6 take pity on
7 take a risk
8 take care of
9 Take no notice

c 2 e, 3 c, 4 b, 5 h, 6 g, 7 a, 8 f

d Students' own answers

5A

1 VOCABULARY & PRONUNCIATION

a 2 upset, 3 proud, 4 relieved, 5 miserable, 6 lonely, 7 disappointed, 8 homesick, 9 grateful, 10 fed up

b 2 bewildered, 3 horrified, 4 astonished, 5 stunned, 6 delighted, 7 devastated, 8 overwhelmed, 9 desperate

c 2 sick of, 3 scared stiff, 4 shattered, 5 gobsmacked, 6 gutted

d **Stress on first syllable:** desperate, devastated, gobsmacked, grateful, gutted, homesick, horrified, lonely, miserable, shattered
Stress on second syllable: bewildered, delighted, offended, relieved, upset
Stress on third syllable: disappointed, overwhelmed

f Students' own answers

2 GRAMMAR

a 2 hadn't taken, 3 wouldn't have, 4 went, 5 would have, 6 would have been, 7 wouldn't be able to, 8 had known, 9 had, 10 had stayed

b 2 we would / 'd have made a snowman
3 I had / 'd known the water was so cold
4 he didn't get so nervous
5 we wouldn't have missed the last bus
6 you wouldn't get sunburnt
7 they had / 'd read the book
8 I could / would / 'd be able to buy my own flat

c 2 you hadn't gone
3 you would / 'd have had
4 you got lost
5 the others hadn't kept
6 a helicopter would have seen
7 would you do
8 you didn't have

d Students' own answers

5B

1 GRAMMAR

a 2 e, 3 h, 4 b, 5 f, 6 c, 7 g, 8 a

b **Speaker wants sth to be different:** 3, 5, 8
Speaker is annoyed about sth: 2, 4, 6, 7

c 3 my boss wouldn't shout (all the time)
4 I could drive
5 my brother wouldn't use my computer
6 my son wouldn't stay in bed all morning
7 I had Dan's phone number
8 you wouldn't leave the bathroom in a mess
9 I didn't have to work this weekend
10 I had time to read books

d Students' own answers

2 VOCABULARY

a 2 exhausting, 3 disappointed, 4 terrifies, 5 frustrates, 6 amazing, 7 embarrassed, 8 inspired, 9 confusing, 10 thrilled

b 2 impressed, impressive
3 offended, offensive
4 scared, scary
5 stressed, stressful

c 2 delighted, 3 impressive, 4 impressed, 5 scary, 6 stressed, 7 offensive, 8 scared, 9 delightful, 10 stressful

3 VOCABULARY FROM READING

2 underachieve, 3 overheat, 4 overconfident, 5 underreact, 6 overcareful, 7 undercook, 8 overwork, 9 underqualified, 10 underactive, 11 overemotional

4 GRAMMAR

a 2 g, 'd worn
3 h, hadn't eaten
4 c, 'd worked
5 f, hadn't fallen
6 d, hadn't shouted
7 a, 'd brought
8 b, hadn't spent

b 2 I wish I hadn't left my phone on my desk.
3 I wish I had / 'd given my boss the report on time.
4 I wish my girlfriend had called me last night.
5 I wish my friend had invited me to her wedding.
6 I wish we hadn't lost our last basketball match.
7 I wish I hadn't been rude to my mother.
8 I wish my son hadn't woken me up in the middle of the night.

5 PRONUNCIATION

1 that job
2 been, party
3 hadn't bought, shoes
4 stayed, home
5 hadn't told, that
6 hadn't come, motorway

Colloquial English 3

1 LOOKING AT LANGUAGE

2 natural world, 3 challenging place, 4 essential items, 5 real privilege

2 VOCABULARY FROM THE INTERVIEW

2 e, 3 a, 4 h, 5 g, 6 c, 7 d, 8 b

3 THE CONVERSATION

2 potentially risky, 3 a bit of a buzz, 4 take risks

4 VOCABULARY FROM THE CONVERSATION

2 for quite a while, 3 Otherwise, 4 It's not just about you, 5 on a more amateur level

Can you remember...? 1–5

GRAMMAR & VOCABULARY

a 2 interesting young Hungarian
3 will / 'll certainly save money
4 had / 'd been walking for
5 will / 'll be flying
6 will have finished
7 unless it's sold out
8 I wouldn't have got
9 wish you would / 'd
10 wish I had / I'd visited

b 1 b, 2 b, 3 c, 4 b, 5 a, 6 a, 7 c, 8 a, 9 c, 10 b

6A

1 GRAMMAR

a 2 driving, 3 living, 4 used to, 5 used to, 6 being, 7 working, 8 play, 9 used to, 10 would

b 2 cooking, 3 living, 4 have, 5 being, 6 go, 7 looking after, 8 study, 9 using, 10 talk

c 2 got used to working
3 isn't used to sleeping
4 used to wear
5 got used to living
6 used to be
7 got used to using
8 not used to having

d Students' own answers

2 PRONUNCIATION

a 2 used to living
3 used to treat
4 used to have
5 used to share
6 used to carry

b /juːzd/: Sentences 3, 6
/juːst/: Sentences 1, 2, 4, 5

d /s/: course, ice, loose, peace, place, price, race
/z/: cause, eyes, lose, peas, plays, prize, raise

3 VOCABULARY

a 2 blanket, 3 snores, 4 sleepy, 5 sleeping pills, 6 nap, 7 duvet, 8 pillow, 9 insomnia, 10 yawn

b 2 a, 3 b, 4 f, 5 d, 6 c

c 2 have, 3 overslept, 4 fall, 5 sleepwalks, 6 were, 7 feel, 8 snores

d Students' own answers

6B

1 GRAMMAR

a 2 c, 3 a, 4 a, 5 c, 6 b, 7 b, 8 c, 9 b, 10 c, 11 c, 12 b

b 2 reading, 3 to find, 4 to call, 5 ironing, 6 to send, 7 meeting, 8 climbing

c 2 want, 3 to see, 4 to learn, 5 adding, 6 listening to, 7 to buy, 8 go

d Students' own answers

2 VOCABULARY & PRONUNCIATION

a 2 saxophone, 3 bass guitar, 4 choir, 5 flute, 6 violin, 7 keyboard, 8 cello, 9 drums, 10 orchestra

b 2 symphony, 3 encore, 4 mezzo-soprano, 5 chorus, 6 rhythm, 7 concerto, 8 genre

d **Stress on first syllable:** cello, chorus, encore, genre, keyboard, orchestra, rhythm, saxophone, symphony
Stress on second syllable: concerto, conductor, guitar, soprano
Stress on third syllable: violin

e 2 architect, 3 chorus

g 2 chauffeur, concerto
3 paparazzi, photographs
4 soprano, microphone
5 ballet, rhythm

7A

1 GRAMMAR

a 2 b, 3 f, 4 h, 5 d, 6 a, 7 e, 8 g

b 2 might have gone
3 can't have seen
4 might not have heard
5 can't have moved
6 might have fallen
7 must have done
8 might not have read

c 2 We should have filled up at the last petrol station.
3 He oughtn't to have left it on his desk.
4 You shouldn't have bought such high heels.
5 I oughtn't to have stayed up to watch that horror film.
6 They ought to have dressed up for the wedding.
7 It should have gone off at 7.30.
8 She should have taken a taxi to the station.

d Students' own answers

2 PRONUNCIATION

a 2 He can't have got my message
3 What do you think of my new flat?
4 The supermarket will have closed by now.
5 How long have you been waiting?
6 We went to see some friends of ours.

c 2 got, message
3 got, angry
4 booked, table
5 been, asleep
6 forgotten

3 GRAMMAR IN CONTEXT

2 would / 'd rather not cook tonight, if you don't mind
3 would you rather do: stay in or go out
4 would / 'd rather we got a taxi home, if that's OK with you
5 would / 'd rather see that film at the cinema than on TV
6 would / 'd rather sit by the window than next to the aisle

4 VOCABULARY

a 2 mind, 3 avoid, 4 Remind, 5 argue, 6 borrow, 7 notice, 8 win, 9 wait, 10 raise, 11 advise, 12 refuse, 13 lie, 14 steal

b 2 lent, 3 beat, 4 robbed, 5 denied, 6 lay, 7 rose, 8 discussed, 9 prevented, 10 expected, 11 mattered, 12 realized, 13 warned, 14 hoped

Answer Key

7B

1 GRAMMAR

a 2 looks as if
3 smells
4 tastes like
5 sounds as though
6 feel like
7 tastes as if
8 seem
9 going out
10 sound like

b 2 sounds like, 3 looks like, 4 smells as if / like, 5 tastes, 6 feels as if / feels like, 7 sounds, 8 seem, 9 smells like, 10 looks as if / looks like

c 1 feels, smells, tastes
2–4 Students' own answers

2 VOCABULARY

a 2 knee, 3 calf, 4 nails, 5 elbow, 6 wrist, 7 thigh, 8 brain, 9 hip, 10 kidneys, 11 chest, 12 heel, 13 palm, 14 liver, 15 waist, 16 bottom, 17 fist, 18 heart, 19 lungs

b 2 c, 3 m, 4 i, 5 a, 6 e, 7 g, 8 k, 9 j, 10 l, 11 f, 12 d, 13 b

c 1 kneel, 2 wave, 3 stare, wink, 4 point, 5 yawn, 6 hug, stretch, 7 scratch, 8 frown

d 2 hugged, 3 frowned, 4 chewed, 5 stretched, 6 knelt, 7 pointed, 8 waved, 9 winked, 10 yawned, 11 scratched

3 PRONUNCIATION

a 2 b, 3 k, 4 l, 5 c, 6 h, t, 7 h, 8 t, 9 s, 10 g, 11 w

c 2 whose, 3 cupboard, 4 foreign, 5 wrong, 6 calm, 7 knife, 8 scissors, 9 autumn, 10 island, 11 what, 12 plumber

e 2 honest, 3 design, 4 autumn, 5 whose, 6 calm

Colloquial English 4

1 LOOKING AT LANGUAGE

2 mind, 3 eager, 4 wary, 5 stead, 6 regard

2 VOCABULARY FROM THE INTERVIEW

2 hang me out to dry, 3 rehearsals, 4 adaptation, 5 have a good ear, 6 mind was blown wide open, 7 prove yourself, 8 audition

3 THE CONVERSATION

2 Probably, 3 However, 4 Also

4 VOCABULARY FROM THE CONVERSATION

2 in short, 3 black and white, 4 to life, 5 so wrong

Can you remember...? 1–7

GRAMMAR & VOCABULARY

a 1 big-headed, 2 hooded, 3 Basically, 4 changeable, 5 stressful, 6 impressive, 7 overslept, 8 frustrated, 9 lay, 10 conductor

b 1 a, 2 b, 3 b, 4 a, 5 c, 6 c, 7 c, 8 a, 9 a, 10 c

8A

1 VOCABULARY

a 2 burglary, 3 burglars, 4 break into, 5 steal

b 2 murder, 3 bribery, 4 stalking, 5 vandalism, 6 blackmail, 7 hijacking, 8 drug dealing, 9 terrorism, 10 hacking, 11 theft, 12 fraud, 13 robbery, 14 mugging, 15 smuggling, 16 kidnapping

c 2 murderer, 3 stalker, 4 vandal, 5 blackmailer, 6 hijacker, 7 drug dealer, 8 hacker, 9 rapist, 10 thief, 11 fraudster, 12 robber, 13 mugger, 14 smuggler, 15 kidnapper

d 2 robbed, 3 stalked, 4 smuggled, 5 bribed, 6 mugged, 7 committed, 8 burgled, 9 murdered, 10 stole, 11 blackmailed, 12 hijacked, 13 dealt, 14 kidnapped, 15 vandalized, 16 hacked

e 2 catch, 3 committed, 4 arrest, 5 question, 6 charged, 7 judge, 8 jury, 9 court, 10 accused, 11 witnesses, 12 evidence, 13 proof, 14 acquitted, 15 verdict, 16 punishment, 17 sentenced

2 PRONUNCIATION

a 2 community, 3 future, 4 punish, 5 guilty

3 GRAMMAR

a 3 had been stolen
4 be caught
5 questioned
6 visited
7 has / 's just been arrested
8 is / 's being held
9 will be heard
10 expects
11 be given
12 will be stolen

b 2 have our burglar alarm tested
3 have / 've had my car repaired by a mechanic
4 had our windows broken
5 will / 'll have my carpets cleaned
6 has / 's had his computer hacked
7 has his flat cleaned
8 are / 're having our garden redesigned

c 3 is expected to be acquitted
4 are reported to have taken the president's wife
5 thought that the terrorists are hiding in the countryside
6 known that the suspect is dangerous
7 said that the police have arrested three men
8 are reported to have damaged several buildings in the area

d Students' own answers

8B

1 GRAMMAR

a 2 eating, 3 to give back, 4 visiting, 5 to dance, 6 of committing, 7 to take, 8 to give, 9 not to be, 10 stealing

b 2 insisted on going
3 suggested going
4 offered to make
5 warned us not to park
6 apologized for being
7 invited Sarah to have dinner
8 reminded me to sign

c Students' own answers

2 PRONUNCIATION

a **Stress on first syllable:** offer, order, promise, threaten
Stress on second syllable: admit, advise, agree, convince, deny, insist, invite, persuade, refuse, regret, remind, suggest

c 2 refused to, 3 threatened to, 4 promised to, 5 agreed to, 6 apologized to

3 VOCABULARY

a 2 wed, 3 fall for, 4 quiz, 5 back, 6 hit, 7 rush, 8 vows, 9 rows, 10 split, 11 bids, 12 clash

b 2 agony aunt, 3 critics, 4 commentator, 5 reporter, 6 editor, 7 presenter, 8 freelance journalist, 9 newsreader

c 2 objective, 3 censored, 4 sensational, 5 accurate

4 VOCABULARY FROM READING

Can be trusted: legitimate, reliable, reputable
Can't be trusted: exaggerated, improbable, misleading, untrustworthy

9A

1 GRAMMAR

a 2 to, 3 even though, 4 in order to, 5 Although, 6 so as not to, 7 in spite of, 8 so that, 9 though, 10 for

b 2 in spite of its ideal location / in spite of being in an ideal location / the fact it was in an ideal location
3 so that they could sell more products
4 in order not to miss my train
5 although I was very late
6 despite being the manager

2 VOCABULARY

a 2 consumer, 3 brand, 4 campaign, 5 jingle, 6 slogan, 7 advertising agency, 8 podcast, 9 spam, 10 pop-up

b 2 close down, 3 branch, 4 recession, 5 boom, 6 drop, 7 manufacture, 8 merge

c 2 markets, 3 produces, 4 imports, 5 has / 's expanded, 6 exports, 7 growing, 8 become the market leader, 9 take over

d 2 makes, 3 doing, 4 made, 5 make, 6 did, 7 made, 8 make, 9 doing, 10 make

e 2 a, 3 d, 4 b, 5 e, 6 f, 7 h, 8 g

f Students' own answers

3 PRONUNCIATION

2 transport, 3 increase, 4 decreased, 5 progress, 6 permits, 7 produces, 8 refunds, 9 imports, 10 records

9B

1 GRAMMAR

a 3 ✓
4 a pair of scissors
5 some cheap accommodation
6 some bad news
7 glass
8 ✓
9 good behaviour
10 some paper

b 2 are, 3 are, 4 is, 5 are, 6 is, 7 are, 8 is, 9 are, 10 is

c Students' own answers

2 VOCABULARY

a 2 post, 3 auto, 4 mono, 5 over, under, 6 mega, 7 multi, 8 bi, 9 anti, 10 mis

b 2 careful, 3 waterproof, 4 useful, 5 homeless, 6 bulletproof, 7 drinkable, 8 hopeless

c 2 weakness, 3 absence, 4 vandalism, 5 Loneliness, 6 racism, 7 childhood, 8 entertainment, 9 improvement, 10 accommodation, 11 distance, 12 brotherhood

d 2 death, 3 heat, 4 width, 5 hunger, 6 loss, 7 height, 8 thought, 9 strength, 10 success

3 VOCABULARY FROM READING

2 monitor traffic, 3 going on every day of the week, 4 digital skills, 5 committed to becoming a clean city, 6 are unmatched

4 PRONUNCIATION

a **Stress on first syllable:** friendliness, government, ignorance, poverty
Stress on second syllable: bilingual, convenience, excitement, reduction
Stress on third syllable: entertainment, overcrowded, unemployment

Colloquial English 5

1 LOOKING AT LANGUAGE

2 had their day, 3 get into your head, 4 a captive audience, 5 word for word

2 VOCABULARY FROM THE INTERVIEW

2 their ears perk up, 3 earworms, 4 passé, 5 pixelize, 6 baton, 7 courant

3 THE CONVERSATION

2 a, 3 c

4 VOCABULARY FROM THE CONVERSATION

2 d, 3 a, 4 b, 5 c

Can you remember...? 1–9

GRAMMAR & VOCABULARY

a 1 has been studying
2 climbing (very) much
3 had his number
4 get used to living
5 looking forward to seeing you
6 never forget visiting Florence
7 must have left your jacket
8 looks as if Emily
9 had our shower fitted
10 encouraged him to enter
11 Despite leaving home late
12 a new pair of shorts

b 1 as, 2 have, 3 by, 4 is / 's, 5 fact, 6 to, 7 take, 8 spite, 9 Even, 10 at

10A

1 VOCABULARY & PRONUNCIATION

a 2 c, 3 a, 4 c, 5 b, 6 a, 7 c, 8 b

c 2 biology / biological; different syllable
3 botany / botanical; different syllable
4 chemist / chemistry; same syllable
5 genetic / geneticist; same syllable
6 physics / physicist; same syllable
7 scientist / scientific; different syllable
8 zoologist / zoological; different syllable

d 3 drugs, 4 discovery, 5 carry out, 6 prove, 7 clinical trials, 8 volunteer, 9 guinea pigs, 10 clone

2 VOCABULARY FROM LISTENING

2 dissolve, 3 particle, 4 scatter, 5 water vapour, 6 reflect, 7 moist, 8 rotate, 9 gravity

3 VOCABULARY FROM READING

2 genes, 3 avatar, 4 toxins, 5 implants, 6 lithium, 7 bacteria, 8 laser, 9 sensors

4 GRAMMAR

a 2 ✗ Everybody was
3 ✗ Everything went wrong
4 ✓
5 ✓
6 ✓
7 ✗ Most people
8 ✗ All dogs

b 2 None, 3 any, 4 none, 5 no, 6 Any

c 2 neither, 3 either, 4 nor, 5 both, 6 Neither, 7 either, 8 nor

d 2 most, 3 Both, 4 no, 5 any, 6 neither, 7 all, 8 none, 9 either, 10 every

10B

1 GRAMMAR

a 2 a
3 –
4 the, the
5 –
6 a
7 –, –

b 2 the
3 The
4 The, –
5 The, the
6 –, –
7 The, the
8 –

c 3 ✓
4 ✗ at school
5 ✓
6 ✗ at church
7 ✓
8 ✗ at university
9 ✗ gone to prison
10 ✓

d 2 c, 3 b, 4 c, 5 b, 6 b, 7 a, 8 a, 9 c, 10 b

2 VOCABULARY

a 2 d, 3 i, 4 f, 5 g, 6 c, 7 e, 8 a, 9 j, 10 b

b 2 rain or shine, 3 right or wrong, 4 now or never, 5 all or nothing, 6 once or twice, 7 more or less, 8 sooner or later

c 2 sick and tired, 3 By and large, 4 touch and go, 5 law and order, 6 safe and sound, 7 wait and see, 8 now and again

3 VOCABULARY FROM READING

2 gift of the gab, 3 sound bites, 4 orator

4 PRONUNCIATION

a Good morning / and thank you for coming. / I'm here / to talk about / an interesting place to visit / in my country. / I'm going to tell you / about the city of Bath / in the south-west of England. / Bath is on the River Avon, / and it has one of the only bridges in the world with shops on either side. / The city is famous / for its ancient Roman Baths, / which can still be visited today. / It has many beautiful streets, / such as the Royal Crescent / and the Circus. / Bath is full of museums, / independent shops, / and wonderful places / to eat and drink. / The city / is easily accessible from London / by train, / and it is perfect / for a day trip / or a weekend break.

c Students' own answers

d Students' own answers

OXFORD
UNIVERSITY PRESS

Great Clarendon Street, Oxford, OX2 6DP, United Kingdom

Oxford University Press is a department of the University of Oxford. It furthers the University's objective of excellence in research, scholarship, and education by publishing worldwide. Oxford is a registered trade mark of Oxford University Press in the UK and in certain other countries

First published in 2026
2030 2029 2028 2027 2026
10 9 8 7 6 5 4 3 2 1

ISBN: 978 0 19 414519 0

Printed in China

MIX
Paper | Supporting responsible forestry
FSC® C109093
FSC www.fsc.org

ACKNOWLEDGEMENTS

The authors would like to thank all the teachers and students round the world whose feedback has helped us to shape English File.

The authors would also like to thank: all those at Oxford University Press (both in Oxford and around the world) and the design team who have contributed their skills and ideas to producing this course.

Finally very special thanks from Clive to Maria Angeles, Lucia, and Eric, and from Christina to Cristina, for all their support and encouragement. Christina would also like to thank her children Joaquin, Marco, and Krysia for their constant inspiration.

The authors and publisher are grateful to those who have given permission to reproduce the following extracts and adaptations of copyright material: p.72 Extract from a speech by 'Oprah Winfrey's 2018 Golden Globe Speech', © Harpo. Courtesy of Harpo, Inc. Reproduced by permission; p.23 Adapted from 'Trading Places' by Stephen Tilden, 2 May 2022, from 50-Word Stories, https://fiftywordstories.com/. Reproduced by permission; p.23 'Generation Gap is adapted from 'Tempus Fugit' by James O'Connor in Mini Sagas by Brian Aldiss (ed.), © Telegraph Media Group Holdings Limited. Reproduced by permission; p.22 'Love At First Flight' by Roberta Beach Jacobson, 14 June 2023, from 50-Word Stories, https://fiftywordstories.com/. Reproduced by permission; p.22 'Evolution' by AJ Joseph, 23 June 2022, from 50-Word Stories, https://fiftywordstories.com/. Reproduced by permission.

Sources: p.67 United Nations World Population Prospects 2024

Illustrations by: Matthew Hollings; Willie Ryan.

Pronunciation chart artwork by: Ellis Nadler.

Video stills: Digeo Productions.

The publisher would like to thank the following for their permission to reproduce photographs: Alamy (PA Images, Andrew Eaton, rosmi duaso, David Askham, UPI, Tetra Images, FITNESS PEOPLE by VISION, Simon Balson, dpa picture alliance, Keith Morris, Dinodia Photos, Lebrecht Music & Arts); Getty (FG Trade, Julien McRoberts, Tetra images RF/Blend Images/JGI/Jamie Grill, kali9, Caiaimage/Paul Bradbury, wilpunt, Capuski, Toby Burrows, Owen Franken, Dorling Kindersley/Dave King, Jason LaVeris/FilmMagic, George Pimentel/WireImage, MJ Kim, E+/JazzIRT, Hiroyuki Ito, simonkr, zeljkosantrac, Luis Alvarez, Paul Drinkwater/NBC Universal, Digital Vision); Science Photo Library; Shutterstock (Atstock Productions, SNEHIT, mavo, Alexxndr, Jurik Peter, spaxiax, Faraz Hyder Jafri, SeventyFour, Lightguard, LarsZ, Dreamfinity Ltd, Vetal, Javen, Vitaly Karyakin, Iakov Filimonov, Linda McKusick, Halfpoint, haveseen, Alexey Sizov, Muk Photo, Monkey Business Images, AJR_photo, Romrodphoto, I Wei Huang, Brian Goodman, urbazon, Rawpixel, Prostock-studio, AnnaStills, aapsky, SpeedKingz, Anton Gvozdikov, ThirtyPlus, M-Production, lovelypeace, LightField Studios, Just Life, Kateryna Onyshchuk, Premreuthai, Ground Picture, Sergey Smolentsev, David Varga, Bobex-73, Sergey Mironov, Lenar Nigmatullin, oliveromg, Jes2u.photo, Tyler Olson, Dmitry Bunin, VGstockstudio, Sabphoto, siamionau pavel, Irelee, posztos, Greg Dale, Tetra Images, Triff, Dario Sabljak, Horiyan, Ferenc Szelepcsenyi, Artur Didyk, Tala-Natali, encierro, B-D-S Piotr Marcinski, astarot, Irina Kuzmina, Volodymyr Plysiuk, grafvision, Voraorn Ratanakorn, Tamara83, Steven Frame, sozon, Dean Drobot, cristovao, ShotPrime Studio, photobank, BearFotos, sima, Lucian Coman, Gorodenkoff, Rose Marinelli, 4kclips, Kritsana Karakate, Olena Yakobchuk, KOTOIMAGES, Stock image, Elenamiv, Thinglass, Paolo Bona, 4045, trekandshoot, peachananr, Radiokafka, PeopleImages/Yuri A, Diyana Dimitrova, alice-photo, Johnathan Esper, Wesley Aston, Yiistocking, Hadrian, GaudiLab, Ground Picture, Monkey Business Images, Minerva Studio, fizkes, BearFotos, Pheelings media, moshimochi, cktravels); Shutterstock Editorial (Depo Photos Via Zuma Wire, Austral Press Agency); Wilderness Bushcraft Society.